c/id

LAURENCE KING

Published in 2006 by Laurence King Publishing Ltd
71 Great Russell Street
London, WC1B 3BP
United Kingdom
Tel: +44 20 7430 8850
Fax: +44 20 7430 8880
e-mail: enquiries@laurenceking.co.uk
www.laurenceking.co.uk

A catalogue record for this book is available from
the British Library.

ISBN-13: 978-1-85669-408-7
ISBN-10: 1-85669-408-9

Printed in China

c/id

Visual Identity and Branding for the Arts

Edited and designed by Angus Hyland / Pentagram
Text and interviews by Emily King

Laurence King Publishing

Contents

Introduction
Angus Hyland

This book is principally concerned with the design and application of visual identity for a selection of organizations in the international culture industry. But first, it may be worth reflecting on what we mean by the 'culture industry' and also by 'visual identity'.

Culture is most commonly used to describe artistic activity and the works produced by it, but it can also be described as social behaviour aggregated in common experience – as in the arts, beliefs, institutions and all the other manifestations of human work and thought. These, together with their attendant attitudes, customs and behaviour, may characterize a particular period, community or attitude, such as Victorian culture, music culture, Chinese culture or the culture of luxury.

A typically contemporary idea of culture comes from composer and artist Brian Eno. He describes culture as 'everything we don't need to do'. We all need clothing, but we don't especially need clothing with colour, ornament or pattern; those parts of clothing are 'culture'. The products of applied art and design can be viewed as cultural because not only do we need them physically, we crave them intellectually. For example, the primary function of a chair is to give you something to sit on. Its secondary function is to be aesthetically pleasing or challenging, and in this it shares common characteristics with its non-functional (unnecessary) fine-art relation: sculpture.

The arts, both public and private, are often represented as the cultural sector of the economy, or the 'culture industry', which works in collaboration with designers and provides them with a platform for experimental and challenging design. This involvement, however, is becoming less and less to do with the patronage of crafts. Institutions such as museums, finding themselves challenged by dwindling public funding and more exposed to market forces, have become increasingly hard-nosed in order to attract and retain bigger audiences and private funding. Particularly across Europe and the US, this has led to the adoption of a more focused and market-driven approach to the way the institutions promote themselves, employing specialist consultancies to 're-brand' them as attractive destinations.

As a result, a museum visit is often more like shopping, with the emphasis placed on 'experience' rather than content. Brand consultants Wolff Olins, responsible for a high-profile re-branding of the Tate Galleries in Great Britain in 2000, describe this shift in focus: 'Tate is brand-led rather than institution-led. Tate offers an open, forward-looking experience, which is as much about entertainment and enjoyment as it is about culture and art.'

This kind of thinking, borrowed from commerce, depends heavily on the method of seduction known as 'lifestyle'. The branding techniques used have been criticized as superficial or voguish and, quite often, at odds with the very content they are meant to promote. However, they do reflect the fact that all organizations throughout the non-commercial world of education, charities and sport, as well as the arts, must now compete more earnestly to attract their audiences.

So what do we mean by 'branding' and how does that differ from 'visual identity'? Designers, in particular, are often sloppy about these definitions, partly because of the ever-changing semantics of marketing jargon and partly because their purposes are sometimes better served by a certain ambiguity.

Designer and author Michael Beirut, in describing an identity, says: '[it] tends to refer to literal identification, specifically to the characteristic way a company or institution writes its name and the rules that govern that characteristic signature. So this is generally a symbol or logotype and all the rules that govern its use.' This is the commonly accepted definition of corporate visual identity and its core application, and it can also be extended to encompass the visual management of the various promotional activities that a company engages in.

Branding now includes all of the above but extends its experience further and deeper – into environments, sounds, smells and attitudes. It is 'total identity', if you like. Used effectively, the power of modern branding can transcend corporate visual identity. If you remove, say, the Apple logo from one of its products or the Nike swoosh from its advertising and can still recognize the source, it is the power of 'brand recognition' that is being demonstrated.

Until quite recently, the word 'brand' referred simply to the trademark or badge that identified a product or manufacturer; the term itself deriving from the branding irons used to burn marks into the hides of livestock in order to identify ownership. Regardless of how we think of the modern usage of branding, it is still fundamentally about identifying. All organizations, groups and institutions have an identity – just like people. It is made up of 'who you are', 'what you do' and 'how you do it'. Successful visual identities employ design to reflect the first two and to help govern the behaviour of the third.

Galleries, museums, art centres and theatres are all destination points and, therefore, their identities are often closely associated with their architecture and their environments. Many of the following case studies – such as The New Art Gallery Walsall and the Mori Art Museum – are prime examples of this. Other identities present institutions by indicating programme rather than location – 'dancing' typography at the Centre National de la Danse in Pantin, for example – while other design programmes, such as M/M's for Théâtre de Lorient, distinguish the institution by introducing visual languages previously alien to local (and in some cases national and global) populations.

Although restricted to a limited number of case studies, *c/id* presents a relatively broad cross-section of projects, representing institutions both large and small to provide an overview of identity systems designed in recent years. While the majority of the following case studies are concerned with institutions in the plastic arts, there are also a number of exceptional examples from the dramatic arts, as well as several cultural centres that embrace a variety of arts practices. The 'culture industry' is one that continues to grow apace, and if *c/id* proves one thing, it is that this particular area of identity design continues to meet the challenge and engender fresh and engaging solutions around the world.

What's this business about culture?
Emily King

Part One

Negotiating the Corporate Model

Culture is a nebulous term. By common consensus, the more of it we have the better off we are, but, closing a lexical circle, it is often defined as that which enriches our lives. Do we benefit from it because it is culture, or is it culture because we benefit from it? In a market economy, culture is often regarded as something that needs extra-market support, a flow of money not generated by the prevailing system of supply and demand. It may be good for us, but as consumers we are not prepared to spend enough to guarantee its survival. This view is common among the governments of Western nations and, to a greater or lesser extent, they all spend money on what they regard as culture.

This spending is not comprehensive, however, and, more and more, cultural institutions are behaving like corporations. This is particularly true in the arts, both the visual arts and performance, where it has become commonplace for institutions to create well-designed, coherent identities for themselves with the aim of attracting both audiences and funding. Alongside these design innovations, they are employing savvy CEO-style directors, marketing experts and micro-managing administrators. The leaders of arts institutions are now required to combine good taste and flair, with a talent for raising money and a certain degree of parsimony. (Unsurprisingly it is rare to find an individual who combines all these qualities, and tensions at the top of arts institutions are not unusual.)

This development has been particularly noticeable since the late 1990s, but it is part of a longer-term trend. In Britain the Thatcher governments of the 1980s undermined the assumption that the extensive public funding of culture was desirable. This led to the introduction of admission charges at some formerly free-of-charge institutions and a few desperate stabs at

marketing. Most notorious of all was the Victoria and Albert Museum's 1988 'Ace Caff with a Quite Nice Museum Attached' campaign produced by Saatchi & Saatchi. Unsurprisingly this slogan did little to assuage negative public feeling about the Museum's introduction of a hefty 'voluntary' admission charge three years earlier. Attendance at the Museum had plummeted and morale among the staff was very low.

There's nothing wrong with modern art that a good cup of tea won't cure.

V&A An ace caff with quite a nice museum attached.

Poster from the V&A's 1988 'Ace Caff...' campaign by Saatchi & Saatchi

Since then things have improved markedly. Whatever we might feel about the shift from public to private funding for arts institutions, Britain probably benefited from being at the helm of these developments. According to artist and former Tate trustee Michael Craig-Martin, "We have an advantage in the fact that we went through that Thatcherite business earlier. The same kinds of problems are happening everywhere, in Germany and in France. There is no escaping these issues, there is a certain amount of historical inevitability."

The V&A has restored free admission and now concentrates its efforts on courting private sponsorship and charging admission for some temporary shows. Of course, corporate sponsorship raises questions about the maintenance of curatorial independence, but these concerns can be offset against rising attendance and a strong exhibitions programme. Even those who view the private funding of culture as a pact-with-the-devil affair, would have to agree that the institutions are at least learning to extract more from the deal.

Audiences and Accountability

The motives of an identity-adopting arts institution are not simple. As well as attempting to offset shortfalls in government funds, they are also trying to meet the demands of a twenty-first-century audience. There is a pragmatic assumption that culture must compete with other forms of entertainment (an assumption shared even by those who don't believe that culture is entertainment). It is generally accepted that an institution with a smart identity and some snappy advertising is in the best position to hold its place in the ever-expanding line-up of contemporary entertainment. Also pertinent is the question of accountability. Institutions receiving public funds must prove that they are able to attract audiences – preferably new, more diverse audiences – to culture. The value of money spent on culture is calculated in an increasingly exacting manner and a highly visible identity

Olafur Eliasson's Weather Project at Tate Modern

is viewed as evidence of a will to compete for visitors.

In spite of the growing range of alternative activities, there seems to be an increased appetite for the arts. In Britain this is particularly true of the visual arts, with visitor numbers for institutions such as Tate Modern reaching all time highs. These visitors are, however, arriving with raised expectations. The 2003/2004 Olafur Eliasson Weather Project installation in Tate Modern's Turbine Hall set the bar for the kind of experience that new art audiences demand.

Events like this become part of a cycle in which spectacular shows generate large numbers of visitors, which in turn generate the need for more spectacular shows, which in turn generate larger audiences and so on. The more success an arts institution has in behaving like a corporation, the more it is required to continue behaving that way. It is not possible to adopt business practices in the short term, as a one-shot means of appeasing the accountants. The corporate model requires a wholesale institutional and philosophical shift, a transformation that brings both gains and losses. The benefit to artists of working in well-run, popular institutions is obvious, but smooth professional practice will always curtail a degree of idiosyncrasy and flair.

Levels of public funding for culture vary widely from country to country. In 2000 a survey found that the United States government spent $6 per capita on culture, where the German government spent $87, the French $57 and the British $27. There are a number of problems with these figures, not least that these countries place very different things within the category of culture (for example, Britain is the only nation to include zoos in the cultural count), but they do reveal a broad picture of varying attitudes toward cultural spending. What they disguise, however, is the converging acceptance of a business model for culture. The German government may spend a fortune relative to America, but the embrace of corporate culture in the arts is becoming near universal. In Britain the current administration loves to talk about the achievements of the cultural sector and the for-its-own-sake need for the arts, but behind the scenes it is slowly chipping away at the edifice of public support. These days only the most efficient institutions are being rewarded with funds. Whatever its absolute merits, these days culture is obliged to prove itself in market terms.

Interior of the Guggenheim Las Vegas

The GuggEnron

If there is a single cultural institution that embodies misgivings about the corporate model it is the Guggenheim. Under the directorship of Thomas Krens, the New York museum has turned itself into a global franchise, opening 'branches' in Bilbao, Venice, Las Vegas (a Rem Koolhaas-designed space inside a casino) and Berlin (on the ground floor of a bank), while it actively seeks new sites worldwide. Krens's strategy is to use the brand leverage of existing Guggenheim concerns to open new ventures, sharing the financing with local organizations and benefiting from the revenues. The Guggenheim bubble appeared to be bursting early in 2002 when the poorly-visited Las Vegas branch was threatened with closure after only a couple of months. Although Las Vegas does remain open, in recent years the volume of noise made by Krens has decreased considerably and plans for other Guggenheim outposts, notably those for a spectacular Jean Nouvel-designed building in Rio de Janeiro, appear to be stalled. Writing in the *Village Voice*, in February 2002, art critic Jerry Saltz called Krens's institution the 'GuggEnron'. The implication was that the director's hubris was overriding concerns about artistic content and curatorial integrity. Outside the United States the museum franchise has been accused of cultural imperialism, attracting the tag of McGuggenheim.

One of Krens's most controversial moves was to stage a show of the work of the fashion designer Giorgio Armani, while at the same time allegedly accepting a donation from Armani of $15 million. The exhibition was poorly received and the museum was accused of allowing the prospect of financial gain to influence its curatorial policy. Krens continued to defend Armani as a suitable subject for an exhibition, but for many this episode is emblematic of what happens when sponsors are allowed to overstep appropriate bounds. The media mauling that Krens received stands as a warning to all ambitious, corporate-minded directors.

Whose Muse?

Between October 2001 and June 2002 a number of major international museum directors delivered lectures under the auspices of the Harvard Program for Art Museum Directors and the Harvard University Art Museums, called 'Art Museums and the Public Trust' (the papers were later published by Princeton University Press as a volume titled *Whose Muse?*). These lectures amount to a defence against the over-enthusiastic pursuit of the corporate model. Of course, American museum directors such as Philippe de Montebello of the Metropolitan Museum of Art and Glenn Lowry of the Museum of Modern Art have always assumed the need for private money, but they argue that the public's trust in their institutions can only be earned by maintaining a barrier between commercial and curatorial activity. The anti-hero of many of the lectures is, unsurprisingly, Thomas Krens.

Invoking the notion of institutional integrity, a number of *Whose Muse?* contributors insist that art museums must pursue goals that are not accountable to empirical measures such as visitor numbers. The book's editor James Cuno (who, at the time he hosted the series, was the Director of the Harvard Museums, and is now Director of the Art Institute of Chicago) argues in favour of the most traditional of museum experiences – that of the unmediated communion between viewer and object. He describes anything that might impinge on that experience – including the elements of identity design that are the subject of this book – as clutter. Although Cuno's description of the meeting of art and its audience is extremely attractive, I can't help feeling that the quality of the encounter that he describes is one that most of us need some help in achieving.

Public vs. Private

Far from being a matter of concern only to museum directors, anxieties about the corporatization of culture have also been raised by academics and cultural commentators. In the book *Culture Incorporated: Museums, Artists and Corporate Sponsorships* (University of Minnesota Press, 2002), Mark Rectanus examines the way commerce shapes the cultural experiences that are available to us. His conclusion, broadly speaking, is that cultural institutions ought to make full disclosure of their commercial interests. Rectanus's position is fairly moderate, and extremely so if compared to that of *New Left Review* contributor Chin-Tao Wu. Wu's data-rich volume *Privatising Culture: Corporate Art Intervention Since the 1980s* (Verso, 2000) asserts that all links between commerce and culture, disclosed or not, are pernicious, and her standpoint begs the question of whether there has ever been an entirely uncompromised system of funding the arts.

Certainly in Britain the notion that public money promotes free and unhindered cultural expression is not one that those responsible for filling in Arts Council forms would recognize. The emphasis on accountability within funding bodies of this kind often creates an untenable burden on the artist or curator, suffocating worthwhile projects at the outset. Even more worrying than stultifying British bureaucracy, however, is the idea that arts spending might become subject to suspect political motives. Certainly many arts institutions in Austria felt uncomfortable receiving money from a government led by Joerg Heider's ultra-right-wing Freedom Party.

All in all, it seems unlikely that there ever was or ever will be a time when public money did not arrive with some political strings attached. It may even be the case that private sponsorship allows for more artistic and curatorial freedom than its state run equivalent. The benefits that corporations receive from their association with cultural activity are often fairly nebulous and it is not usually in their interest to attempt to dictate the activities of artists and curators. Of course, there is the Guggenheim's Armani incident, and highly controlling sponsors who attempt to use the arts as a means of inflecting their image in a very particular fashion do exist, but private money in itself is not evidence of inappropriate input from the commercial sector.

A Third Way

Miguel Zugaza, Director of the Prado Museum in Madrid, is exploring new avenues for the funding of building work and exhibitions. Where formerly the Prado was almost entirely maintained by the Spanish government, Zugaza has begun to bring in sponsors to support its higher profile activities. Fully aware that these moves could be controversial, he is very specific (in the interview that appears in this book) about the Museum's priorities: a curatorial programme based on scholarship and expertise first, and fund-raising second. Zugaza emphasizes that the most important elements of the Prado's identity are its astonishing permanent collection and its eighteenth-century building. Viewing the issue from a particularly national standpoint, he points out that museums have become an important element of national and civic identity in post-Franco Spain.

The other interviewees in this book also promote what could be described as Zugaza's public/private middle way. American graphic designer Michael Rock questions whether there was ever a time when funding for cultural institutions was 'pure'. In spite of their apparent ties to corporate or private money, he praises American arts institutions for being some of the last remaining places where Americans can enjoy a relatively non-commercial experience. Michael Craig-Martin concurs, welcoming the new audience that has been brought to contemporary art. Tate Modern has had a strong curatorial programme since it opened in 2000, but it is undeniable that the crowds have been encouraged by the museum's very visible identity and its active marketing campaign. Craig-Martin admits that traditionalists may complain about the manner in which these new visitors engage with art, but as far as he is concerned this criticism is somewhat surly. It seems there is a consensus in the interviews that arts institutions must, to some extent, behave like corporations. The purpose of this book is to explore how corporate practices, specifically the practice of identity design, can best be tailored to meet their needs.

Event Architecture

The case studies in this book deal mainly with the graphic elements of identity, but of course this is only one part of a more complex picture. Considering museums worldwide, the icons that spring to mind tend to be architectural not graphic. These include not only recent museums, such as Tate Modern and the Bilbao Guggenheim, but also older structures, such as the original Guggenheim in New York or the nineteenth-century Museum Island complex in Berlin. The effect of spectacular architecture in drawing an audience and kick-starting broader urban regeneration has been well documented. There are sceptics (in particular there are many who question the long-term benefits of the Bilbao effect, both specifically in Bilbao and in other cities such as Newcastle), but for the time being 'event architecture' remains a popular strategy for cultural institutions.

The Serpentine Gallery has taken a particularly ingenious approach to this trend. Based in a classical 1930s tea pavilion in the middle of London's Hyde Park, the gallery has little scope for permanent expansion. Instead it raises a temporary structure on its lawns every summer, each one designed by a renowned architect. Where 'event architecture' is often criticized for being unsuited to day-to-day use, the Serpentine scheme has the advantage of allowing architects to construct buildings with the sole purpose of creating an event.

The Social Whirl

The Serpentine uses its temporary pavilion for a number of purposes, the most prominent being the gallery's annual summer party. Drawing hoards of celebrities and featuring in the social pages of publications such as Vogue, this party has, in itself, become an important part of the

Serpentine's identity. Its status as a fixture on the London social calendar was cemented when Princess Diana was pictured arriving at its precursor, a fund-raising dinner, held in June 1994. This kind of event remains fairly unusual in British arts circles, but in the United States fund-raising galas are commonplace. The mother of them all is the Metropolitan Museum's Costume Institute Ball, a grand party that draws the most glamorous stars decked out in their finery. Not only does this gala raise enormous sums of money, it also wins the museum acres of coverage in everything from the fashion press to the daily newspapers.

Other arts institutions take a more democratic approach to marketing themselves through their events. PS1 in Queens, New York, holds its openings on weekend afternoons/evenings, bringing in live music and DJs. Tate Modern staged a much promoted series of art, dance, theatre, film in the spring/summer of 2003. Even those institutions without a high-profile events programme tend to be running educational activities, including lectures and workshops. As well as being worthwhile in their own right, these happenings are the material through which the institution constructs its identity. Contemporary museums and galleries often aim to offer their audiences all-round, multi-sensory experiences: at their worst these constitute distracting clutter, but at their best they can enhance the audience's encounters with the arts.

Content First

The case studies in this book cover the conventional ingredients of corporate design: a logo; house-style typography; a colour scheme and so on. By and large they are designed by an external design team and then later applied in-house by the institution. These schemes are all effective, but they could not be used to disguise poor programming or bad art. For an identity to be successful, it must have its roots in the purpose and achievements of the institution, particularly at the moment when its implementation transfers from the original designers to an in-house team. Grafting a fancy design onto an uninteresting or badly run museum, theatre or gallery is not going to fool anyone in the long term, particularly not the institution's own staff. What you will find here are instances of good design working to promote rich, productive endeavours.

The majority of the examples are centres for the visual arts, although there are also several interdisciplinary institutions and theatres that promote innovative dance and performance, as well as more traditionally-staged plays. This bias toward the visual arts reflects a high level of awareness of design among the staff and stakeholders of these institutions and it is hardly surprising that art museums and galleries tend to think very carefully about the graphic language in which they present themselves to the public. That said, looking at the best of the theatre projects, such as the identity and advertising for Shakespeare's Globe Theatre in London, it is obvious that graphic design is as relevant to performance as it is to the visual arts. Drama audiences are just as attuned to appealing advertising and a coherent identity system as those for other forms of culture.

Most of the arts spaces discussed over the following pages are non-profit-making concerns. This includes both institutions that rely on public money and those that are privately funded. The case studies do, however, include three examples of commercial outfits. In each case these were chosen because of their will to use design to communicate with an audience broader than their immediate customer base and they all keep regular hours

Exterior of Shakespeare's Globe Theatre with promotional posters in the foreground

when they are open to visits from members of the public. Cynics might argue that this desire to communicate is simply part of a longer-term strategy to appeal to buyers. Possibly it is, but if it means that we benefit from seeing good art in thoughtful environments, then so much the better.

All the case studies but one come from Europe or America, the exception being the Mori Art Museum with an identity designed by Jonathan Barnbrook. Discussing this imbalance, Barnbrook suggests that Japanese arts institutions tend to be more academically focused and

Interior of the Mori Art Museum in Tokyo

influence our perceptions of the arts and, in turn, influence the way arts institutions choose to present themselves to us. The current level of interest in the arts is unprecedented and this is reflected in the ebullience of the identity design that has emerged in recent years. The arts may have to take their place in the line-up of entertainments, but at the moment they are doing so with justified confidence.

Other factors in the mix include possible shifts in the practice of identity design. To date the logo remains a key element, but it seems likely that graphics will evolve beyond this formula. The designer Nick Bell anticipated this development in an article titled 'Brand Madness' published in autumn 2004's *Eye* magazine. Exploring the landscape of arts identity design in London, Bell questioned whether cultural institutions truly need all-embracing, logocentric identities. Arguing that it is often more appropriate to allow design for culture to be determined by content, he suggested that we should welcome the diversity and inconsistency that such an approach might imply. This idea is attractive and it credits arts audiences with a great deal more intelligence than does the application of more homogenous systems. (An example of this method, and a personal favourite, is the *Newspaper Jan Mot*, an intelligent, content-driven publication designed for a small Belgian gallery by the Dutch designers Maureen Mooren and Daniel van der Velden.) This post-logo understanding of identity is not confined to cultural institutions, but it will suit them better than most.

However sophisticated and sensitive identity design becomes, there will always be those who regret the developments that have encouraged arts institutions to behave more like corporations. And they will be right, of course, that these changes have implied losses as well as

also have a less international curatorial programme than their European and American counterparts. As a result, museum and theatre directors in Japan may not feel the need to reach out beyond their traditional audiences or to carve out worldwide reputations for their institutions. It will be interesting to see whether this situation changes in the next few years. For the last decade or so galleries and museums in Europe and America have been encouraged to view their success as a global phenomenon, and chances are that institutions across the world will start to follow suit. Certainly the international attention received by the Mori is unprecedented for a Japanese institution, and this is likely to encourage its immediate competitors to bid for a more cosmopolitan profile (graphic and otherwise). A survey such as this made in as little as five years time might have a very different geographical emphasis.

Of course, the potential for change in the subject area mapped by this book is not confined to geography. There is a vast range of political, social and cultural factors that

Two issues of the Newspaper Jan Mot, designed by Maureen Mooren and Daniel van der Velden

gains: marketing will always favour the generalist above the expert. But feeling nostalgic for a time when there were fewer cultural institutions, and when each of them was less well visited, is retrogressive. An institution that combines promoting itself with integrity and skill with the maintenance of a worthwhile programme deserves to be rewarded with visitors and funding. This survey includes many such examples, and I believe, case-by-case, its contents are cause for optimism.

Interview

Michael Craig-Martin/Artist

Emily King: What was your role in the branding of Tate?
Michael Craig-Martin: You mean the Wolff Olins proposals?

Well that, but also the building and the whole new Tate identity.
So you are talking about a much larger thing than just the product branding. Well, I became a trustee quite soon after Nick [Serota] became director, in 1989/90. I remember that it was obvious that, as Trustees, we were going to be looking at expanding the museum, which was desperately needed. There was already an existing plan by James Stirling, who had designed the Clore Gallery. I thought it was terrible; it took up most of the remaining original site without meeting the museum's needs.

Feasibility studies were done, looking at how much the site could be redeveloped, how much space could be created. The conclusion was that a certain amount of expansion was possible on the site that is now Tate Britain, but this would never be adequate in terms of the Tate's long-term needs. At that point a very important decision was taken by the Trustees. We realized we had to find a new site and build another museum.

When was that decision taken?
In the early 1990s. Then there were several studies done with regard to where the museum might go. It could have been anywhere! We looked at all sorts of places.

Did people raise the question of identity in a self-conscious way during those discussions? Were you thinking of a Tate-like site?
No, not so much that. But I think we all felt very uneasy about the idea of dividing the museum and how we would then define what went on at each site. Were we creating an entirely new museum? What about the collections? All of those questions came up and there were many, many discussions before decisions were made.

The Tate at Millbank, now known as Tate Britain

So it wasn't necessarily going to be a Modern/Britain split from the start?
I can't remember when that distinction became clear. There were certain considerations, one of them being that the collection is British through the whole of British history and modern since the beginning of 1900. It is not quite so clearly defined, but more or less. Then there was the very odd relationship with the National Gallery. Essentially the reason that twentieth-century art isn't in the National Gallery is because, during the twentieth century itself, it wasn't considered good enough. That's why it ended up being shunted into the Tate, which was already a museum of British Art.

But, as the century went on, certain early twentieth-century pictures began to be considered quite wonderful and the National Gallery was in the position of simply saying, 'well, we'll have that'. That's why Seurat's *Bathers* is in the National, though it was originally in the Tate. The National Gallery could just cherry pick.

When did that change?
The relationship between the two museums changed during the restructure of the Tate.

So it was possible for the National Gallery to behave in this way until 2000?
Yes, at any moment the National Gallery was still in a position to say, 'we'll take Matisse's *Snail*'. There was no clear delineation about where its collecting stopped.

Once the construction of Tate Modern began, the Tate and the National Gallery came to an agreement, which was essentially that the National Gallery would collect more or less up to 1900 and the Tate would collect more or less after 1900. A significant number of works were exchanged between the two galleries on this basis, although they remain part of the collection of their original gallery. Monet is a good example: most of his work is nineteenth century and therefore at the National, whereas his *Waterlilies* is twentieth century and has been moved to the Tate Modern. I personally think Tate Modern should be seen as the National Gallery II, it is the equivalent of the National Gallery for the twentieth century and beyond.

The National Gallery and the Tate identities are so different, I have never seen them that way.
But if you think about it, it's very clear. It leaves Tate Britain as a national museum, essentially the equivalent of the Whitney in New York.

The other thing that, as an artist, I think is very

sensible, although I know a lot of artists who disagree, is that the collection was kept as a single entity. The Tate has four museums, Liverpool, St Ives, Tate Britain and Tate Modern, but there's only one collection, which the curators from any one of the four institutions can draw on. If the collection had been divided, the people who would have suffered were potentially the British artists. If the collection had been divided, only some British artists would have been represented in the Tate Modern collection. Maintaining a single collection has meant that any post 1900 British artist, now or at any time in the future, can be exhibited in Tate Modern.

Why don't artists like that?
Let's face it, there is a sense that Tate Modern, because it is international, is more prestigious than Tate Britain. There is a big question about retrospective exhibitions for British artists. The Tate has insisted that all British artists have retrospectives in Tate Britain, no matter how international they are, no matter how important, whether it is Lucien Freud or Bridget Riley, which seems reasonable to me. There was a point at which it seemed like some people might be shown at Tate Modern and some at Tate Britain, and that would have opened a can of worms. But, back to the identity, it was really a case of firming up areas of typical English vagueness, which were causing more and more problems. Obviously Nick didn't want to sit there waiting for the National Gallery to decide that they were going to pluck out some of the best things, so now we have a national museum dedicated to the twentieth century and beyond.

When did the branding proper start, with the discussion of the name and so on?
That was very late in the day, when the building was nearing completion. It was an interesting process because it involved such a comprehensive overview.

During the entire period of planning and construction, I had always called the buildings Millbank and Bankside. I really expected the name of the location to be included. But what came out of the branding exploration was that the name Tate was itself the brand. It is recognized all over the world and is immensely powerful. This simplification is a very contemporary kind of branding, the abbreviation through removing the definite article.

At the start it was very odd saying Tate rather than the Tate, but I am surprised how quickly I became used to it.
I know I thought 'I will never say it, no one will ever say it'. Then, I couldn't believe it, within a week of it being announced, you would hear people on the radio referring to Tate Britain.

Do you think it might become dated?
The branding that existed before was the branding of a particular period, and the branding of Tate Modern and Tate Britain is the branding of another. Of course it is of its time.

Do you think it will change?
I doubt it, but I do think that there are fashions. We don't call the National Gallery 'National', but then it hasn't been reformulated. Wolff Olins made the re-branding of the Tate part of a whole rebirth. It announced that it isn't the same institution, and it's not just the new bit that has changed, the old bit has changed too.

Do you think the branding could have done more for the old bit, Tate Britain?
There were people who worried that Tate Britain would suffer. But it needn't, it is just a question of using its role properly. Many people who come to Britain have heard of Young British Art and they want to see it. I believe there should always be a substantial amount of contemporary work on show at Tate Britain.

But they don't own a lot of it, do they?
They own more than you might realize. Of course there are lots of things they should own that they don't, but they could borrow pieces. I think it is very disappointing at a time when contemporary British Art attracts a lot of attention, how little there is on show.

What do you think of the appearance of the Tate identity design?
There are things that I like about it and things I don't. It is a corporate programme, created by people who are used to dealing with businesses. I was amazed at the sophistication of it, the attention to detail. There is a set of rules that govern everything from the tiniest memo notepaper, to the sign on the side of the building. This is obviously very powerful, because it means that the sense of identity is being reinforced at every opportunity.

Do you think it is necessary for arts institutions to have that kind of identity?
It is very pronounced at Tate, but that is partly to do with its vastness as an institution. The branding was meant to overcome the sense of fragmentation.

Do you ever have misgivings about the branding of the arts in general? Do you ever suspect that branding obscures content?
There is an analogy here with those who think that if you want to get on in the art world you have to know the right people. Of course it can't hurt, but if your work isn't worth seeing, knowing everybody on the earth isn't going to make a lot of difference. It is the same with branding. It draws attention to you, but, if you don't deliver the goods, then branding is not going to save the day.

Tate Modern at Bankside

Do you think promoting art in a manner that is derived from the corporate world could ever create problems?
Well, we've been through a transformation in the way the world works. I spoke to someone who had been a trustee, maybe in the late 1970s or early 1980s, and she asked me if I was enjoying the role, whether it was interesting. I answered that it was fascinating, and I was very lucky because it was an amazing time to be a trustee, but the only depressing thing is that we spend so much time thinking about money and fund-raising. And she said, 'You discuss money! I was a trustee for seven years and I don't remember discussing money once!' In her day, the purchase grant in relation to the price of art was sufficient that, if they wanted to buy a Picasso, they bought a Picasso. Of course they couldn't buy everything, but they had a budget that matched the prices. By the time I became a trustee, much of the art that we wanted would have cost the entire budget.

These days there's pressure about money and pressure about audience, plus the fact it's all monitored. Nobody used to care how many people went to a museum until recently, until the government started asking whether these institutions are 'paying their way'. These are corporate considerations and you can't afford not to take on corporate methods when you are adopting the same values.

Is this a change for the worse? Does it stop things happening at Tate that might be of value?
I don't think you can have any change without a combination of loss and gain. You always lose something, there is no doubt about that, but there is also no doubt that we've gained fantastically in terms of our capacity to show things. For example the Olafur Eliasson piece at Tate Modern, it's an amazing phenomenon, ordinary people are flooding to see it.

I am reluctant to feel nostalgic. The England that I came to [from America] in 1966 has disappeared without trace. Of course there were things I loved about it, that's part of the reason I stayed, but I also have to say that there were things about it that were ghastly. I don't sit around wishing it were 1966 again. I don't think that there is any country that is more transformed.

Do you think we are destroying museums as contemplative spaces?
Well, they are crowded with people. One of the reasons Tate and the National Gallery are at times unbearable is because they run such extensive education programmes,

they are filled with children and young people, but is one going to say this is a bad thing?

Moving on from institutions, what about the more contentious notion of artists as brands? Do you think that this idea is becoming more prevalent?
I can certainly see what you mean by that, sure, and I am conscious of it. Obviously Picasso was a brand, using today's language. Fame is now seen as branding. To become famous at something is to build brand recognition, and once you have brand recognition you can do all sorts of things.

Do you know any artists who self-consciously pursue branding?
Well, I always assume that someone like Tracey [Emin] must understand it. Tracey is genuinely interested in celebrity. She loves the idea of being famous and will do things that draw attention to herself and build brand recognition.

Do you think that this is detrimental to the notion of art, or the making of art?
Well, again, these are cultural inevitabilities. There used to be an idea that high art, to use a term that you don't often hear anymore, was above the nitty gritty, that it existed on a more rarefied plane. It was an aspect of modernism's willingness to be disdainful of popular acceptance, but that has gone now.

Of course there is a sense that art has been compromised in some way. But remember, in the 1970s nobody in Britain was interested in contemporary art. We weren't just doing it for ourselves, we believed it had a social function, but there was no audience. The same people who were complaining about a lack of audience in the 1970s are now complaining about dumbing down.

If your audience is 200 incredibly committed and sensitive people whose lives are devoted to knowing your work in depth, and then you increase that audience to 2 million people, you are going to get an entirely different level of engagement. Now, we have a big audience with much less knowledge and commitment. But why did we ever think that it wouldn't be like that?

Miguel Zugaza/Director
Museo Nacional del Prado

Emily King: What do you think are the most important elements of the Prado's identity?
Miguel Zugaza: Above all, the pieces that form the collection, and also the building, which is the work of the eighteenth-century architect Juan de Villanueva.

You have recently instituted the 'Paseo del Arte' in Madrid, a route that takes in several museums including the Prado. Can you tell me more about this development?
In the 1980s the Prado was the only museum in the area. Then, in 1988, the Reina Sofia [Museo Nacional Centro de Arte Reina Sofia] opened in the space that used to be the eighteenth-century General Hospital, and four years later a site was found for the Thyssen Museum [Museo Thyssen-Bornemisza]. It was a political decision to concentrate a series of cultural institutions in this area, around the Prado.

Why did this grouping happen?
Well, I think it's a strategy that has been followed all over the world. There have been several cases in which institutions have been clustered, principally to share their audience. [Historic examples include London's South Kensington museums, established in the mid-nineteenth century, or Berlin's Museum Island, founded in the early nineteenth century and currently under-going extensive restoration. A more recent example is Vienna's Museum Quarter, opened in 2001.] Roughly 1,700,000 people visit the Prado Museum, but, together with the other museums, the Reina Sofia and the Thyssen, visitor numbers rise to more than 3,500,000. It benefits the museums, but, above all, it benefits the public. It creates a more convenient and accessible way of celebrating culture and art.

Also, since Spain regained democracy [in 1975] there has been a strategy of using culture as a tool for social development. I think that the Socialist government came

Main entrance to the Prado's original building, now augmented by a vast extension

up with this strategy of uniting cultural institutions because it was a way of showing the world Spain's new commitment to culture and art.

It strikes me that, as an institution, the Prado is very bound up with the Spanish national identity, much more so than, say, the National Gallery in London. Would you agree?
The Prado is a distillation of the long history of Spain. We have made it accessible to the public, but it remains a museum whose historic value is crucial, like other historic collections, such as that in Vienna or the Hermitage, for example.

Are you trying to communicate the idea of national identity in the new identity for the Museum?

No, the new identity relates to the Museum's mission of cultural communication. The Prado represents a national identity because it unites all of Spain's major historic schools of art, but the new identity concerns the Museum's global mission of communicating the value of excellence.

So, above all, you are trying to communicate yourselves as an international museum?
Yes. Without doubt.

Are you trying to attract a new audience to the Museum?
Until now the Prado Museum has fulfilled the missions that it undertook when it was founded – that is, to preserve its collection, to study it and to restore it – but we've made very little effort to open the Museum to society and to communicate the value of its contents. That is a subject we must address. We must be more open to different kinds of visitors, be much more democratic in that sense. It's not enough just to open the doors, which is what we have been doing. We have to commit ourselves to reorganizing the way the Museum communicates with the public.

The Prado, the Reina Sofia and the Thyssen are three very different museums. How will they be related to one another?
When the 'Paseo del Arte' is finished it will be easier for the visitor to understand the relationship between the activities of the three museums. For instance, an extraordinary, but not well-known, feature of the Paseo is the Botanical Garden. It was designed by Juan de Villanueva while the Museum was being built.

So you can walk through the Botanical Garden to get from the Prado to the Reina Sofia?
Yes, the idea is that it will act as a promenade.

Promotional banners for the Prado's Manet exhibition lining the Paseo del Arte in Madrid

Will you try and make the museums more uniform in nature? For example, at the moment the guards' outfits in the Thyssen look like those of airline stewards, while those at the Prado look much more municipal. Is this something you intend to address?
No, some differences should be preserved, the Prado is a public museum, an official museum. But when we get closer to finishing the extension and making the changes we have in mind, we might work on a new uniform, to transform the personnel of the Museum.

There is a lack of balance between the excellence of the old masters in the Prado and the relative weakness of the 20th century collection of the Reina Sofia. Is that something you will try and rectify?
The Reina Sofia is an attempt to make up for a century of failing to collect contemporary art. There is a great void at the heart of its collection, but fortunately this began to be rectified the moment the Museum was founded. Adding to the Reina's collection is a very important task.

The history of contemporary Spain has lost something that was very important for the collection in the

Prado, and that is a dialogue with international artists. The Prado collection reflects the fact that Rubens was working in Spain and that Titian worked for Charles V [who was both the Holy Roman Emperor and the King of Spain]. What the Prado collection reflects is a universal vision. This is in sharp contrast to modern times, the nineteenth and twentieth centuries, when Spain isolated herself from significant international schools of art.

Do you think that it is a problem that public museums are forced to act more like private corporations?
No, but one has to know how to do it well. A museum like the Prado will continue to receive the greater part of its funding from the government, but it should also be responsible for providing part of its funding itself, through selling tickets, services or products, or through private societies and private companies that help develop its programmes. I think you can do this perfectly well without selling yourself or presenting yourself in an overly corporate manner.

I am against corporate interests affecting the policies of the Museum. I think you have to avoid that. But if someone wants to share the prestige of the Prado, and if it's good for the project... The private sector comes in only when the Museum has decided its needs, once it has determined the programme. Then we turn to a few select benefactors, each with a lot of money, rather than opening ourselves to any kind of patronage.

Do you have private benefactors?
We have a foundation of 'friends', but they don't deal directly with the Museum, instead they are a private foundation.

So it's very different from the American model, where museums receive a lot of money from individuals and families?

It's another culture. Europe is not America, and Spain is hardly even European. I personally defend the idea of public museums. I think it is important that so many of Europe's cultural institutions are public institutions, contributing to the national identity and the character of public life. They are like great hospitals promoting public health, they are one of the most significant services that the state has to provide. A museum director can dedicate 10% of his time to obtaining external funding for its activities, but if it takes up 50% of his time, that's bad. A director of an American museum generally has to dedicate 60 or 70% of his time to getting funds. That is the reason that they have great difficulty finding directors for their museums.

Nicholas Serota had to spend a great deal of his time raising money for the recent Tate building.
Yes, but Nick, along with the other great British museum directors, is launching an appeal to the government saying that the administration must show more solidarity with cultural aims. The British public museums have an important quality, which is that they are free. It gives them a legitimate cause to demand that the administration should treat them generously.

Is there a particular museum that you see as a model?
Specifically, I look at the National Gallery in London. Its experience over the last ten years provides a clear example, both with regard to the great degree of autonomy that it has acquired and, on the other hand, its manifesto to return the museum to the public. As well as very high quality programming, they have a clear vision of how to reach their audience. I think that Neil MacGregor, who is now at the British Museum, has very much left his mark in this area.

The National Gallery has begun to show contemporary art, can you imagine doing something similar?

Yes, of course. I think the experience in London in that sense has been very positive. It is important to break the conventional division between the art of the past and contemporary art. That does not mean that the Prado has to become a museum of contemporary art, rather it has to make a series of proposals explaining the relationship between the collections and the contemporary. A few weeks ago we had an exhibition dedicated to Manet called 'Manet in the Prado'. Although set in a nineteenth-century context, in some ways it was akin to an exhibition of a contemporary artist engaged in a dialogue with the collections. It serves as a prototype of what the Prado can do, showing how the Museum can relate to the art of the vanguard.

Do you worry that overt marketing will turn the jewels of your collection into advertising images? For instance, if Las Meninas is used in 'branding' will it be seen as a piece of publicity rather than a work of art?

The problem is that we cannot control this process. There are a million products that use Las Meninas, but none of them are related to the Prado. The Prado uses the image of Las Meninas in only a few products, but the image has been set free. There is no way to control it. The Director of the Prado is surprised every time he returns to Madrid and sees an advertisement in Barajas airport showing Las Meninas with a mobile phone. We haven't authorized this image, but all we can do is laugh. The image is universal.

Is something lost when an institution such as yours aligns itself with the corporate world?

I don't think the Prado is going down the road of turning into a corporation and therefore I see no risk. Rather than a vision of commercialism, I see the creation of good service for the visitor, which, aside from exhibitions and the collections, means that there are shops and restaurants. The idea of the museum experience is very current, and, rather than isolating ourselves, we must find a place in contemporary society.

I think the commercialization of the Museum is also an element of our communication and we have to ensure that it is an instrument that is used to the full. For example, until now we have controlled only our Museum shops, but we should be entering much larger circuits of distribution. It would strengthen the cultural communication of the Museum.

It's odd that the Prado, which has three paltry little shops on site, is reproached for a commercialization. I think that it's a reproach that could be made of a lot of museums, but not of the Prado. At the Tate, for example, the first thing you see when you enter is a huge shop, while here at the Prado, if you want to find a postcard, you really have to search for it.

It seems that Spanish museums are often sites of controversy. Why is that?

I think it has to do with the recent socio-economic and political history of our country. Spain has just woken up to democracy and the speed of its social development has been incredible. The conflict is due to a very accelerated process of modernization and inevitable questions about Spain's position on the world stage.

Spanish museums have become emblems of the process of modernization and democratization. These days nearly all the autonomous communities, the regions and cities, are using museums — or the architecture of museums — as marks, as symbols of modernization. It's very strange that it should have turned out like this. In many places museums arrived before high-speed trains!

Michael Rock/Graphic Designer
2x4/New York

Emily King: Does designing for cultural institutions require a particular approach? Are there particular considerations in designing for culture?

Michael Rock: You can look at that question from two different directions: one: does the work need to be different because it is a cultural institution rather than a commercial one? And, two: is there something about the organization of cultural institutions that makes working for them different?

In my experience, notions of hierarchy and inclusion are quite different in cultural and corporate environments. While corporate clients are comfortable with clear hierarchies and chains of command, cultural institutions often seem to be more invested in inclusivity. Even while the director might have absolute power, there is a desire to be sensitive to the rank and file. The process tends to be much more about consensus building.

Does that kind of view go for the audience as well? While a corporate client might have an idea of a hierarchy of consumers, with the wealthiest at the top, a cultural client will take a much more democratic view?

Design for cultural institutions is directed at the public in a very broad sense, rather than at a demographic market. Of course cultural institutions have demographics, but they tend to see their mission in broader terms. For instance, we have just finished work for the Brooklyn Museum. It is the second largest museum in America in terms of its collection, coming in right behind the Metropolitan Museum of Art, but in terms of audience it is completely different. Brooklyn is probably one of the most diverse communities in the world. The Museum had to imagine their public mission in a very different way than, say, a corporation which is selling very specifically to eighteen-year-old boys.

Also, in general there is an altruistic aspect of a public organization. The work isn't meant only to define or package the audience as a market segment. That brings me to the other part of my question: 'Does the work itself have a kind of quality?' I think it does in that it has the aspect of a public offering, it should be a gift to the public as well as a device to sell to them.

The public realm has become very finely graded in that there are now state-run museums and privately run cultural institutions and various shades in between. Do you try and reflect these types of ownership and control in your identity designs, or disguise them?

I don't think we're actively disguising. It usually happens in more natural way. When you are working for privately run cultural institutions, you are dealing with people who are already concerned with the aesthetic, people who see themselves as active players in culture. Relating to these issues, even when museums take a more commercial approach to branding, for instance the Guggenheim, which has become a franchiser developing a worldwide network of museums, it is still a cultural reaction to a commercial phenomenon. It is an example of cultural institutions realizing that they need to be part of commerce and to comment on it simultaneously. When a museum adopts a highly branded approach there is necessarily a level of commentary as well.

So you think that culture still makes sense as a category, even though it has an increasingly leaky boundary with commerce?

Yes it does, not least because cultural institutions don't have nearly the budget or the level of exposure of big commercial clients. Ideas that might work for BMW or Nike, designs that would create a consistent message through sheer exposure, will not work for cultural institutions. Most museums don't have one-hundredth, even one-thousandth of the advertising budget of a company like that, so they are relying on a much smaller number of impressions to create their image. It is a much more limited way of revealing yourself to the world.

You mentioned that the Metropolitan Museum has a very different audience to the Brooklyn Museum. Do these institutions use design to try and change the nature of their audience, to make it younger for example?

To a certain extent, but while a big public museum needs to be aware of its audience, it doesn't segment in the same way a commercial client does. The function of design for a commercial client is to create an audience that defines itself as a user of that product. For most cultural institutions that is still a fairly alien notion. They are public institutions and they want to be as broadly inclusive as possible. Their audience is limited purely by people who are interested in and love art. While, of course, all the contemporary critique is true – that museums have to sell things in order to survive, and they have to have corporate sponsorship and so on – at the heart of it, they are still organizations that demand nothing of the user other than that they show up and pay their $10. They don't have to buy things in the bookstore or even have a cup of coffee, the market is very broad that way.

Are you simply trying to expand the audience?

All museums want to increase visits, that's what proves they're doing well. That means they have to create shows that appeal to certain markets, or they have to make their experience more pleasurable. They are trying to appeal to changing tastes in the market. Museum directors want to go to their boards and be able to say they increased visitor figures by 30% last year, or show increases in memberships, or simply bring in more cash.

But there is a reaction against this kind of thing, blockbuster backlash …

Right, you get a lot of shows that people have problems with because they see them as dumbing down, or appealing too coarsely to popular taste. There is a big debate around all of those things.

The Director of the Art Institute of Chicago, James Cuno, describes all design and marketing, including shops and cafés, as clutter; things that come between the viewer as the object.

Any gesture toward accessibility is seen as clutter, as dumbing down, but I think that there is an argument to be made from the other side. For a long time art museums have limited their audiences to the affluent, white middle classes and part of the dumbing down argument is about maintaining that status quo. If you want a broader audience, with different expectations of museums and different backgrounds, then you have to create different kinds of experiences. I don't buy the purity argument, it seems to be somewhat classist and racist. I personally like the pure museum experience, but I am not sure that it's the best experience or the only experience you can have in relation to art.

Whose views come first in your design for cultural institutions: audiences, artists, curators, trustees even?

It is a typical design project, you always have a divided and multiplied audience, although maybe it is even more complex in a museum. You are dealing first and foremost with the public who use the museum, but then you have the artists who show there, the curators, the board of trustees, the director and his or her staff. Ideally everyone keeps the absolute end in mind, but this is often not the case. The public are probably the last people to notice the design, but ultimately it must function for them.

Have your designs been subject to focus groups?

Not so much in the museum context, it is more typical for them to have gone through some kind of branding exercise before they approach us. But I have yet to find one of those that is that useful. They are usually full of suggestions that you could probably have thought up on your own if you had had a couple of minutes, such as people don't like to go to the Brooklyn Museum because it is in Brooklyn! The result is usually along the lines of 'our goal is excellence' – pretty generic statements.

Do you personally regret the developments that have made cultural institutions behave more like businesses?

No, I think it's the nature of our times.

Do you see your input as part of this process?

Absolutely, we are an integral part of that. I tend not to get nostalgic about some time when culture was pure, because I doubt that there was ever such a time. In general, culture doesn't work that way.

Do you use design to distinguish cultural institutions from commercial ones?

To a certain extent, I think that cultural institutions are a bit softer in terms of what they can do. They don't necessarily want to be as crass in presenting their organization and they may be more accepting of certain visual ideas, but these are all generalizations.

Did you ever feel that you are protecting a cultural institution through design?

No, in my experience directors of cultural institutions see them as extremely flexible organic organizations. They are not to be protected, but perfected. We improve on, focus or sharpen, rather than preserve.

Have you ever felt that your work has been compromised by a corporate sponsor?

No, but a lot of organizations we work for are privately funded and that raises interesting questions. For instance we just completed the Nasher Sculpture Center in Dallas, a museum that was paid for by one person. It is an institution that anyone can go to, a gift to downtown Dallas of a sort, but it is sponsored by an individual who has total say on what happens there. Personally, I don't think the public are compromised by that. It was the condition of creating the museum.

Are there any institutions that you do feel are compromised? Many people would cite the Guggenheim …

The Guggenheim is seen as the dark knight of museums and Thomas Krens as a figure who has destroyed culture by the introduction of commerce, but I don't agree. He's operating a kind of experiment, exploring what happens when you use the cultural value of a very well known organization as leverage. I can accept this because I don't believe art was ever pure. It has always been used politically, as status and leverage. High art was first introduced to American consumers through department stores in the nineteenth century. The idea of a pure cultural space is a myth. Conditions are different now, but they are not any better or worse than before.

Have directors and museum boards become more aware of the issues around identity design over the period in which you have done this kind of work?

In general, the overall awareness of identity and branding has increased immensely. I think that this has been influenced by a couple of things. One is the development of the Internet – websites have made people aware that the way something looks is part of the product – and, at the same time, branding started being taught in American business schools as part of the curriculum. Anyone who has been through Harvard Business School in the last fifteen years has had a long, very evolved discussion about the meaning of branding. They will probably have had a lecture from Martha Stewart. Businessmen have become much more aware of the value-adding quality of the visual.

Do you look at other institutions in the field? Do you feel you are placing your product?
Yes, very much so. Over the years we have collected a huge database of information about different cultural institutions, that is part of our expertise. We have a design presentation that starts with an exhaustive survey, encompassing the naming of institutions, their look, how they use colour and typography and so on.

In terms of the Brooklyn Museum, which institutions did you include in your comparative survey?
We started off comparing it to all museums worldwide, looking at 300 different logos. Then we narrowed it down to museums of the city and other museums with encyclopaedic collections. We also looked at different strategies for naming, full names, acronyms and so forth. As a counterpoint, we also compared it to other kinds of institutions that aren't cultural, like Target or Nike.

Are there any of your own cultural identity projects that you would pick out as particularly successful?
Different ones stand out for different reasons. A while ago we did the identity for P.S. 1, which is a contemporary art institution in New York based in an old school building in Queens. I think theirs has been an extremely successful graphic programme. It is really simple and works in a very straightforward way.

In terms of assessing the success of P.S. 1, have you been looking at visitor numbers, or is that too crass a measure?

Exterior shot of P.S.1, Queens, New York City

It is to do with their programming and their use of space. For instance, they realized that most people don't want to go to an opening in Queens on a Thursday night, so they instituted a series of Sunday afternoon events. They have DJs and installations in the yard, attracting thousands of people. It's great to get people into the space who wouldn't normally be there. These are events that are really unique experiences in an art museum.

Is branding a word that you feel entirely comfortable with in connection to culture?
We don't use it, because I am not sure exactly what it means. But in general cultural institutions have boards of directors that are headed by men and women who are running very large corporations and are extremely interested in this issue. They are bringing their corporate experience to museums.

If you are not using the word branding what are you using, identity, communication?
We usually use identity, it's a gentler term.

Signage for P.S. 1 designed by Michael Rock at 2x4

I guess you could say that museums who try to repackage their collections so that people see them differently, reintroduce things to the public that they've had all along, are attempting to rebrand or recontextualize materials. But art doesn't demand anything of the viewer, you don't have to buy anything. You can just look at it, and have your own feelings. It is a much more passive relationship because it doesn't demand a sale at the end. I can hear already the critics who say, well museums are all about the shop now, but you don't have to do any of that stuff, you can go and have your $10 experience and that would be it. Anytime you create a fairly non-commercial public experience, that's a good thing. It is important that art still has the ability to generate experiences that aren't fulfilled by buying.

In another context you said that 'branding was the last attempt of the desperate'. Might that apply here? Does the fact that cultural institutions are turning more and more to branding imply that culture is in some kind of crisis?
Well, what happens often-times in commercial organizations is that you develop a product, the product is doing really well, everyone is into it, and it moves on its own. Then the market becomes saturated, the product has lots of competition and becomes lost in a crowded market.

AMERICAN
FOLK ART
MUSEUM
45 WEST 53RD STREET

AMERICAN ANTHEM IS SPONSORED BY

PHILIP MORRIS
COMPANIES INC.

American Folk Art Museum
New York / USA

Founded in 1961, the Museum of Early American Folk Art opened just down 53rd Street from the Museum of Modern Art. The conviction of the founding trustees was that the work of untrained or self-taught artists ought to be taken as seriously as that of their professional counterparts. The museum began collecting through donation and purchase in 1962, opened its galleries to the public in 1963, was renamed the American Folk Art Museum in 1966 and opened its stunning new premises in 2001, near its original location.

Despite making a number of notable acquisitions and mounting several well-received exhibitions, the museum spent its first decade dogged by financial difficulties. Threatened with closure in 1971, it only achieved relative financial security in the late 1970s under the directorship of Robert Bishop. Unfortunately, however, this economic gain was offset by a period of itinerancy. The museum started the 1980s on 53rd Street and ended it, a couple of moves later, in a storefront space near Lincoln Center. In 1991 Bishop was succeeded by Gerard Wertkin who, as well as pursuing plans for a permanent home, strengthened the museum's holdings of Latino and African American Folk Art. In 1998 Wertkin established the Contemporary Center, a section of the Museum devoted to new work.

In December 2001 the Folk Art Museum opened the doors of its new permanent home, designed by Tod Williams Billie Tsien & Associates. The museum's current graphic identity was launched concurrently with the building. Developed between 1999 and 2001 by Woody Pirtle of Pentagram, it encompasses signage and environmental graphics, as well as promotions, publications and a website. Pirtle's design for the Museum references folk art techniques, particularly that of quilting, a form of art that accounts for some of the museum's most valuable holdings. The logotype is patched together from single-word sections, with the key phrase of the museum's name – 'Folk Art' – running vertically, top to toe. Not only indicative of the museum's collection, the graphic style also reflects its architecture, particularly the distinctive panelled façade.

The materials used in the new building were chosen for their combination of ordinariness and beauty. Each with a distinctive colour and texture, they include the tombasil, or white bronze, of the outside panels, the textured concrete of the interior walls and the reddish Douglas fir used in the detailing. This palette of architectural tones informed the colour scheme of the identity, a scheme consisting of six natural hues to be used in combination with each other, and with grey and black. One of the most pressing demands of both the new building and the identity was that it should meet the needs of the two folk art constituencies: traditionalists and more contemporary self-taught artists. Pirtle's solution was to incorporate iconic objects, both traditional and new, into the identity. Represented in a number of ways – silhouette, mezzotint, halftone or four-colour reproduction – the various elements of the collection coexist in perfect graphic harmony.

Previous spread, left An example of the banners displayed around Manhattan promoting 'American Anthem', the inaugural exhibition at the American Folk Art Museum, in 2001. **This page** Representative images from the collection have been employed as elements of the identity, treated in a range of ways including silhouettes, mezzotints, halftones, four-colour reproductions or outlines, allowing disparate objects to co-exist within the identity. In printed applications like posters (bottom left and right), the two styles of work may be composed in translucent layers. When appropriate, they may appear separately as well, including branded merchandise such as mugs (below left). **Opposite page** The patchwork motif of the logo – inspired by the great American art of the patchwork quilt – is employed as a decorative element across a wide range of applications, from signage to carrier bags from the museum gift shop.

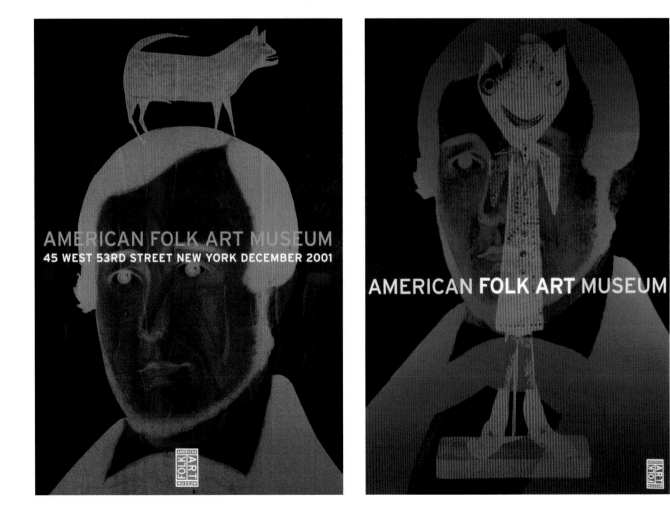

BALTIC: The Centre for Contemporary Art
Gateshead/UK

BALTIC

BALTIC is a centre for contemporary art situated on the south bank of the River Tyne in Gateshead, near Newcastle. Opened in July 2002, it is part of the ongoing regeneration of an area known as Gateshead Quays, a mixed-use programme that also encompasses Sage Gateshead (a Norman Foster-designed concert hall), the award-winning Gateshead Millennium Bridge and various leisure centres.

BALTIC is housed in a 1950s grain warehouse, which was part of the former Baltic Flour Mills. Its development as an art centre is part of a trend (exemplified by London's Tate Modern) of converting industrial structures to cultural use. BALTIC's building was adapted by the architect Dominic Williams, who was inspired by its imposing brick-clad form to preserve its industrial appearance, both inside and out. The centre is extremely substantial, housing five galleries that together amount to a total of 3,000 square metres of exhibition space. Having no permanent collection, BALTIC emphasizes commissions and artist-in-residence projects. Coupled with the nature of its gallery spaces, the programme prompts the metaphor of the centre as a factory for art.

BALTIC's graphic identity was developed in tandem with the structural and functional conversion of the building. The work of Swedish designers Henrik Nygren and Ulf Greger Nilson, in collaboration with founding director Sune Nordgren, its style is consistent with the project's overall aesthetic approach. The core of the identity is a distinctive typeface developed from a 1940s design and now registered under the name 'BALTIC Affisch'. This face is used across the centre's signage, printed communications and website. Its unfussy, wood-block appearance complements the building's architectural palette of brick, aluminium, steel, pine and slate.

Launch director Sune Nordgren was highly involved in the development both of the BALTIC's physical spaces and its visual communications. He worked in consultation with artists, including Julian Opie, who produced site-specific art projects for the centre's immediate environment, and a small range of merchandise to be sold in its shop. The guiding aspirations shared by Nordgren and his team were that the centre should be functional, flexible and honest. To an extent, the simplicity and restraint of BALTIC's architectural and graphic expression sets it apart from the glossier, higher-tech elements of the surrounding riverside development.

Since the centre's launch, Nilson and Nygren's original design has been further developed and extended by a number of freelance and retained design agencies, namely Ripe, Joseph White, and more recently, Blue River, who have collaborated on maintaining and developing the BALTIC brand. The typeface has created a consistent expression for the centre's extensive programme of exhibitions and activities, including educational events, cinema screenings, lectures, a media lab, a library and an archive.

Previous spread, left BALTIC's bold industrial logo, photographed during the transition of the former flourmill into one of Europe's leading centres for contemporary art. **This page** The BALTIC newsletter was a powerful communication tool for the centre between 1998 and 2001, publishing information on a wide-ranging programme of international exhibitions, events and seminars that took place in and around Gateshead before the gallery opened. The final edition of the Newsletter (No.16) was published to coincide with the gallery's opening. **Opposite page** The first edition of the BALTIC Newsletter was published in October 1998, four years before the gallery opened its doors to the public. The photograph on the cover is one from a series of striking images of the old flourmill by Etienne Clément.

BALTIC Centre for Contemporary Art
Opens Autumn 2001 in Gateshead

No.1

Opposite page This tote bag from the BALTIC shop boasts a rare splash of colour. **This page, above left** An A3 fold-out leaflet introducing readers to BALTIC. A dramatic shot of the building's exterior, showing the Level 5 viewing box, suggests the sheer bulk of the building. Presented alongside the BALTIC mark, the image further reinforces the appropriateness of the identity. **This page, bottom** Invitation to the opening of B.OPEN, the inaugural exhibition at BALTIC and an attempt to 'explore the full potential – architecturally and conceptually – of this unique building as a site of encounter between artists, artworks and the visitor'. **This page, right** The BALTIC's typographic language lends itself well to slogans. These beer mats were part of the B4B programme that tied in with Jenny Holzer's 'Xenon' projections (2000). The beer mats were distributed across the region to promote Holzer's projections and furthermore to promote BALTIC, part of the broad pre-opening promotional campaign.

BAM: Brooklyn Academy of Music
New York/USA

BAM

The Brooklyn Academy of Music opened in 1861 and has operated almost continuously ever since. The only prolonged cessation of its performing arts programme occurred between 1903 and 1908 when, after burning to the ground, the Academy was rebuilt on a new site, its current home on Lafayette Avenue. In recent years BAM has made a virtue of its grand, but ageing, beaux-arts premises, becoming a landmark of Brooklyn's heterogeneous and increasingly fashionable Fort Greene district.

BAM's present-day dynamism owes much to its erstwhile executive director Harvey Lichtenstein. He arrived in 1967 at a significantly depleted institution, where language classes were being held in the performance spaces and a school for boys had set up in the ballroom. Lichtenstein embarked on an ambitious, long-term programme of renaissance. By the time he departed thirty-two years later, BAM was internationally recognized as a forward-thinking centre for theatre, music and film. Its facilities include the Howard Gilman Opera House (which also houses a cinema) and the smaller Harvey Theater, named in Lichtenstein's honour, which opened in 1999.

Although BAM has a consistently high critical profile, presenting avant-garde performances by artists such as Robert Wilson and Mark Morris to rapturous audiences, it is constantly seeking to expand its constituency. BAM's best-known programme is the Next Wave Festival, an event season that brings together experimental theatre and music from all over the world. Taking place each autumn since 1981, its reputation is such that it draws crowds to – for many – a previously uncharted neighbourhood in Brooklyn to see unknown acts.

Pentagram's Michael Bierut, designer of the BAM identity, was first brought in to create the graphics for the 1995 Next Wave Festival. Working with colleagues Karen Parolek and Bob Stern, he formulated a consistent look for the printed communication, the hook of which is partially concealed typography. Initially, letters emerged over a series of broad horizontal bands, a metaphor for something new and exciting coming into view. More recently, type has been slightly obscured on the right-hand side, again suggesting something beyond the horizon, but this time relating more to the idea of text and the spoken word. After a single season it became apparent that Bierut's graphic metaphors stood for the institution as a whole and the design was extended, as he puts it, 'pan-BAM'. As well as creating a coherent identity, this allowed the cachet of the Next Wave Festival to rub off on the rest of BAM's activities.

The next stage of the BAM identity came in 1997 when Bierut was asked to collaborate with architect Hugh Hardy in the renovation of BAM's Fulton Street building. The work included the design of wayfinding signs, information kiosks, a donor wall and street signage. This adaptation of the graphic identity to the architecture has been particularly successful. Bierut and Hardy's combination of clean type and elaborate architectural detail is a perfect illustration of the virtues of combining the two- and three-dimensional elements of an institution's identity.

Previous spread, left Signage at BAM's Rose Cinemas (opened in 1998) continues the theme of the core identity, with oversized door numbers positioned in such a way that clarity is retained, even though part of the figure is cut off. This page Emerging text as visual device is especially effective when employed in the building's signage. The designers collaborated with the architect Hugh Hardy on the renovation of the Fulton Street building, developing an effective and cohesive visual language that complements the architecture of the building. Opposite page Exterior signage for the BAM Harvey Theater. The oversized type and dramatic lighting have enhanced the theatre's reputation as one of Brooklyn's premier venues.

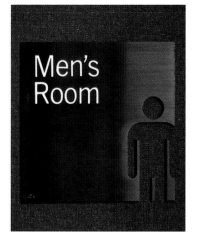

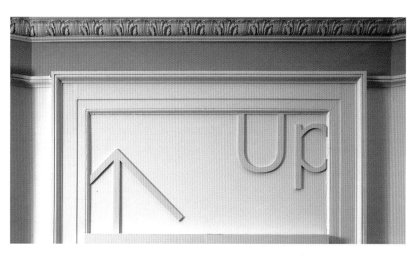

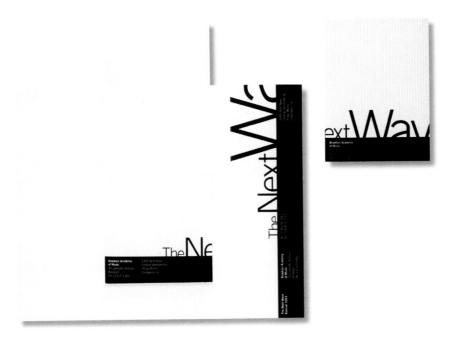

Opposite page Established in 1981 as part of a mission to promote new talent, the Next Wave Festival is BAM's signature programme and it has prompted some excellent print promotion campaigns, designed by both Pentagram and the in-house team. Posters for the 2000 and 2001 event (top) show just two of the visual routes travelled by the designers, while a more monotone palette (bottom) reveals an austere, though no less dynamic, tone. **This page** The cover of the Spring 2000 programme of events communicates both the season and BAM's commitment to promoting emerging talent, with elegant yellow type emerging from a field of green stripes. Rather than resort to a photograph of grass, the designers selected a more abstract approach that reflects the contemporary tone of the BAM identity. The typographic language continues throughout the programme's spreads, with photographs also cropped to create a cohesive whole.

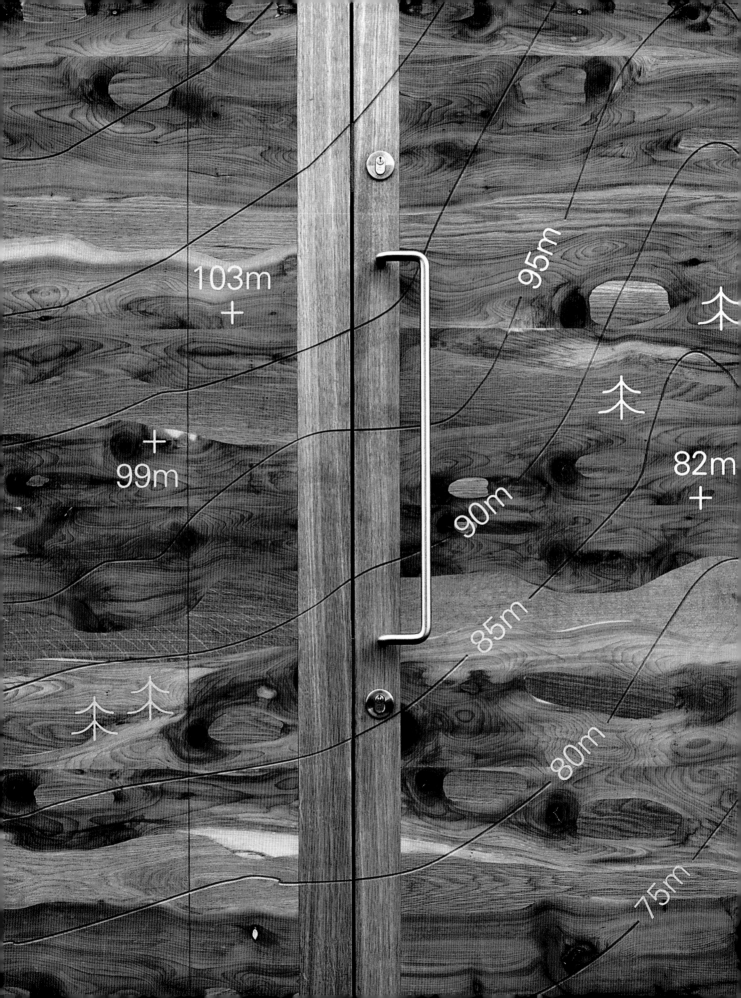

Cass Sculpture Foundation
Goodwood & London/UK

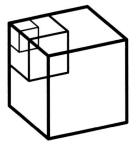

Established in 1994, the Cass Sculpture Foundation was formerly known as Sculpture at Goodwood, and its core activities are based in twenty-two acres of woodlands in Goodwood, West Sussex. By dropping the regional element from its title, the foundation hoped to reposition itself as a more outward-looking, international organization. The foundation's name change in 2002 was followed by the opening of a small urban outpost in London, in 2003.

The Cass Sculpture Foundation was established as a charitable trust with the aim of advancing British sculpture. Its activities include commissioning and funding new work and promoting British sculpture around the world. It has facilitated the making of numerous new sculptures by British artists, enabling many younger artists to work on a large scale for the first time. Cass's rural venue hosts a changing display of British sculpture, charting a course from the beginning of the twentieth century, with an emphasis on recent activity. Meanwhile, the foundation's London gallery has become a display space for maquettes, many of them for newly commissioned works. Designed by Daniel Weil of Pentagram, the dark wood floors and grey walls and ceilings of this converted Georgian building imbue the sculptural works in progress with a sense of drama.

The Cass Foundation mounted its first international exhibition at the Peggy Guggenheim Collection in Venice in 2002. Titled 'Thinking Big', the show explored the sculptural maquette and its recent reappraisal as a work of art in its own right. The current identity of the foundation was launched to coincide with this exhibition. In discussion with the founders and patrons, Mark and Wilfred Cass, the design team Made Thought (Ben Parker and Paul Austin) created a logo that communicated the range of the organization's interests through a play on the notion of scale. The series of three cubes, each one double the dimensions of the last, offers a metaphor for the foundation's concern with every stage of the sculptural process and its will to see a project through from maquette to fully realized work. The typeface is VAG Rounded, a face much favoured for its friendly, playful qualities.

The catalogue for 'Thinking Big' was divided into two separate books, united with a Z-bind. One book showed images of the work with no reference to scale, while the other offered details of the size and materials of the models and the biographies of the artists. Made Thought have maintained the theme of creating graphic interest through unusual folding and binding in subsequent Cass publications. In keeping with the mission of the foundation, they are defining a common territory between graphic design and sculpture.

Previous spread, left The front doors of the London gallery are made of yew, taken from trees grown at Goodwood. The grain of the wood suggests the natural contours of the landscape, whilst Ordnance Survey maps of the Goodwood sculpture park have been engraved and inlaid with stainless steel. **This page, top right** Catalogue designed to present one of the foundation's most famous commissions, Marc Quinn's *The Overwhelming World of Desire* (Paphiopedilum Winston Churchill Hybrid), a twelve-metre-high steel orchid. Made Thought presented the orchid in all its glory, with typography and background colours directly influenced by its vibrant yellow, orange and red hues. VAG Rounded, the core typeface of the identity, again seems an appropriate choice, communicating information with playful clarity. **This page, centre right** Catalogue for 'Thinking Big, Concepts for Twenty-first Century British Sculpture', held at the Peggy Guggenheim Collection, Venice between 2002 and 2004, and organized in association with the Cass Sculpture Foundation. Presented in a slipcase with silver foil-blocked type, the catalogue has two distinct sections, separated by the Z-bind. The typographic language borrows from the core identity, with VAG Rounded allowing for a level of expression and playfulness. **This page, bottom** Promotional leaflet for Tony Craggs' *Chalk Pit*, the first in a series of major 'One Year, One Man' shows at the Cass Sculpture Foundation Sculpture Estate in Sussex. Made Thought designed a sculptural leaflet, with overlapping layers folding out to reveal a more expansive view of the site. **Opposite page** The foundation's gallery in central London is not a conventional white-walled gallery, but a unique venue that presents the creative process involved in making sculpture. Designed by Pentagram, the space was conceived as a theatre, with dark, smoked oak flooring and grey walls and ceilings presenting sculpture and work in progress within an appropriate context. This photograph shows the gallery in its first incarnation, complete with views from and into Focus Gallery. The space has now doubled in size, following the closure of Focus Gallery in 2004.

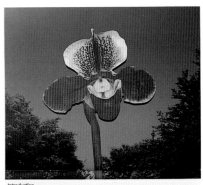

CDDB Théâtre de Lorient
Lorient / France

The CDDB (Centre Dramatique de Bretagne) Théâtre de Lorient is a venue for drama and dance located in the small Breton town of Lorient in northern France. It is part of a network of Centres Dramatiques Nationaux (CDN) maintained across France, largely through public funding. Supporting its own repertory company, it not only plays a significant role in the cultural life of the region, but also tours performances nationally and worldwide.

The town of Lorient suffered badly from the bombardments of the Second World War and was rebuilt during the 1950s and 1960s in an architecturally undistinguished fashion. According to the Paris design team M/M, when they posted their first advertisement for the theatre on the streets of the town in 1996 it was as if a 'very big alien' had landed. The poster's large scale and its dramatic graphic language created a striking contrast with the low-key urban surroundings. Far from appearing extra-terrestrial today, however, the theatre posters have become something of a local event. They are anticipated, engaged with, collected, even studied at neighbourhood art classes.

M/M view the Lorient posters as a progressive project. The only fixed element is the typographic identity for the theatre, a complex three-dimensional affair consisting of an irregular dot-matrix typeface, an assertive set of drop-shadow capitals and a mark, which seems to vacillate between being an inkblot and a flash of light. Around this identity, M/M's visual metaphors for the plays have become more complex, their typefaces less straightforward and their typography more expressive. Many of the elements used in the Lorient posters appear elsewhere in M/M's work. In particular, the designers maintain an archive of photographs, often using a single image in several different contexts (in October 2002 eagle-eyed locals may have spotted a picture of Björk, another M/M client, in a poster for Lorient's production of Marguerite Duras' *Savannah Bay*).

The CDDB poster identity is an ongoing design adventure, a joint undertaking by the theatre and its public. For a long time Lorient's inhabitants fought against the uniformity of their post-war surroundings by painting their houses pastel shades. Now they have the dramatic posters from their local theatre adding to the communal effort to create a distinctive urban landscape. The CDDB took a risk in introducing the distinctive graphic language of M/M to Lorient. It could easily have been interpreted as a Parisian invasion of the regions. That it has instead been embraced as a local asset is testimony to the benefits of not underestimating your audience.

Previous spread, left M/M view the posters they design for the theatre as a 'progressive project', with an ever evolving and broadening palette of visual elements and references. Exhibition view, 'Icônes, Indices, Symboles' Chapelle des Jésuites, Festival International de l'Affiche et des Arts Graphiques de Chaumont. **This and opposite page** Lorient is awash with the eclectic visual language of the posters that promote the theatre, whose productions are highly regarded both nationally and internationally. Rather than conformity, it is innovation that distinguishes the theatre's identity as a cohesive one. M/M's palette of photographs, illustrative elements and typography continues to bear weird and wonderful fruit, such as these posters promoting productions from the 2003–2004 programme.

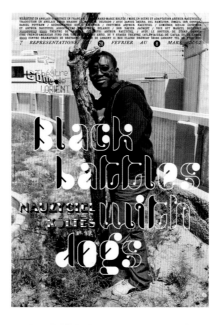

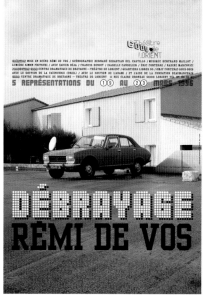

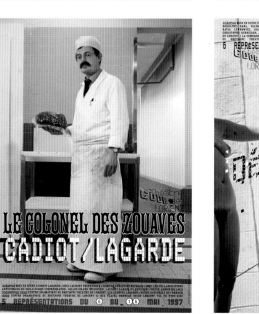

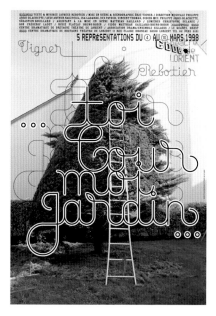

This page Earlier posters, such as these promoting productions in the mid-1990s to 2000 (centre and bottom row), were entirely typographic, although the number and variety of typefaces used prefigures the eclectic image-based language employed in more recent years (top row).

Opposite page The visual language employed for the covers of these annual publications is more restrained than that of the posters. Whilst this paring down may well have been dictated by difference in scale, the designers still employed a broad palette of elements, the only visual constant being the table top on which an array of appropriate objects is placed.

L'ILLUSION COMIQUE
CORNEILLE / VIGNER

CDDB ‹ 2001 ›

CDDB ‹ 2002 ›

CDDB ‹ 2000 ›

CDDB ‹ 1998 ›

CDDB ‹ 2004 ›

CDDB ‹ 1999 ›

ERIC VIGNER BRANCUSI CONTRE ETATS UNIS

CDDB ‹ 2003 ›

Centre National de la Danse
Pantin / France

Inaugurated in June 2004, the Centre National de la Danse (CND) is located in the Parisian suburb of Pantin, just north of the Parc de La Villette. The area is characterized by unprepossessing post-war architecture and the centre itself occupies a Brutalist building designed in 1972 by Jacques Kalisz. Although this concrete structure has impressive qualities, it was never well liked by those in the neighbourhood, not least because it used to house police headquarters, tax offices and courtrooms. Converted by the architects Antoinette Robain and Claire Guieysse, the building now accommodates eleven dance studios – three of which are open to the public – an exhibition space, a well-equipped resource centre and office space for the many dance companies who spend periods in residence. The mission of the CND is to promote experimental choreography and innovative dance education. The atmosphere is more akin to a workshop than a theatre, with the emphasis being on exchange and dialogue rather than performance. Catering to both dance professionals and the community of Pantin, the centre maintains a dual agenda of local and global concerns.

In their conversion of the building Robain and Guieysse took advantage of the large open spaces and the natural light of Kalisz's structure to make a series of elegant public and private facilities. One of the structure's most striking features is a sculptural staircase that is visible through the centre's partially clear façade. It is further emphasized by a dramatic, multi-coloured lighting scheme designed by lighting artist Hervé Audibert. The centrepiece of the CND's identity is a very large sculpture-cum-sign on the roof of the building that was created by graphic designer Pierre di Sciullo. Made from angular pieces of metal, when seen from the correct perspective the sign spells out the simple instruction 'Danse'. Di Sciullo's commanding tone is a humorous reference to the building's previous tenants, and the fact that you might have to move around a little to read the sign is a playful means of enforcing its direction. Financed by the '1% artistique' initiative, under the administration of the Direction Regionale des Affaires Culturelles, the sign has become a local landmark, inspiring new affection towards Kalisz's building.

As well as the supergraphics, Di Sciullo also designed the signage for the interior of the building. Set in a jaunty, sharp-edged typeface that appears to sit on a zigzag baseline, in the case of these signs, it is the letters, not the readers, which do the dancing. Several of the directional signs disappear around corners taking their audience where it needs to go, and many are enhanced by a fleet of arrows. All in all, the effect is one of constant graphic motion: type tip-tapping like dancer's toes.

The logotype for the CND was created by the Paris design team Atalante. Consisting of a double spiral inspired by choreographic notation, it encompasses the form of the initials C and D and also suggests the intertwined movements of a dancing couple. Designing posters for the centre, Atalante combine the logo with adventurous dance imagery. In particular, they are interested in photographing dancers from unusual angles, from above or below. The resulting images reflect the experimental, laboratory environment of the centre as a whole.

Previous spread, left Located just outside central Paris, the Centre National de la Danse in Pantin occupies a Brutalist building designed in 1972 by Jacques Kalisz. The centrepiece of the signage system is the large sign on the building's roof. Designed by Pierre di Sciullo, the sign is made from large pieces of metal and when seen from the correct perspective spells out the simple instruction 'Danse'. **This page, top** Applications of the identity include *Kinem*, a journal designed by Atalante and published twice yearly to brief readers on news and forthcoming events. Imagery, typography and layout again reflect the

energy of dance, whilst the restrained black and white colour palette employed for all the covers gives *Kinem* a consistent language, distinguishing it from other CND publications. **This page, bottom** These posters promoting productions for 2000–2001 combine dynamic images of dancers with animated colour schemes and layouts to suggest the energy of both the art form and the venue. The visual language perfectly complements the bold typography and swirling symbol of the identity. Designed by Paris design studio Atalante – also responsible for posters and other promotional print collateral – the symbol is a

double spiral, inspired by the movements of a dancing couple and incorporating the letterforms 'c' and 'd'. **Opposite page** Interior applications of the signage system designed by Pierre di Sciullo. Three-dimensional signs (top and middle) employ the same construction technique as the large roof sign, albeit on a smaller scale. Elsewhere, signage information is painted directly onto wall surfaces (bottom), complete with dancing typography and clean, angular pictograms. The interior sign system complements the architecture of the building as well as the identity, and communicates information with optimum clarity.

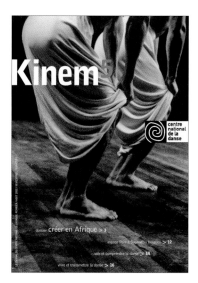

ici niveau 1

foyer des danseurs

Mammalian animals and Mar
Mammiferi e Uomini

Fondazione Querini Stampalia
Venice / Italy

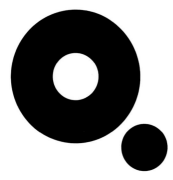

In 1868, on the wishes of the last descendant of the Querini Stampalia family, Count Giovanni, the Venetian Palazzo Querini Stampalia became a cultural and artistic foundation. Today the Palazzo houses a museum of fine and decorative arts from the fourteenth to nineteenth centuries, a well-used library – the oldest holdings of which come from the Querini Stampalia family archive – and several spaces for events and temporary exhibitions. Between 1959 and 1963 the Palazzo was restored by the celebrated architect Carlo Scarpa. Allowing the Venetian tides to penetrate the lower level of the building in a series of elegant canals, and creating a beautiful courtyard garden, Scarpa designed what is widely considered to be his masterpiece. The marriage between the old and the new on the lower levels of the Palazzo is both sensitive and striking, all the more so in the context of Venice, where modern architecture is a rarity.

In summer 2001 the Querini Stampalia commissioned a new identity design from the Venetian design team Studio Camuffo. Sharing a belief that the existing graphics did not offer clear information about the nature of the Querini Stampalia or its facilities, the foundation and the designers agreed to start afresh, creating new materials to promote every aspect of the institution. At the core of Camuffo's challenge was reconciling the need for a single identity for the foundation that expressed the particular character of each of its various elements. They responded with a logo, a uniform typographic system and a colour scheme. These are used consistently across the foundation, the distinction between its activities being made through the choice of hue: information about the museum is offered against a slate blue background, the library is promoted in orange, the architecture in deep red and the contemporary art activities in a green-tinged yellow.

The most visible element of the identity is the logo. A schematic Q formed from a black circle with its middle cut out and moved to its lower right-hand side, thereby creating a tail, the design is highly recognizable. As with Scarpa's architecture, it is even more noticeable in the Venetian context where historicism abounds and clean, simple design is an exception. Since the logo's launch in October 2001, it has appeared on t-shirts and carrier bags, allowing the foundation's message to travel around Venice and beyond.

Previous spread, left The grand fascia of the renovated Venetian Palazzo was brought to life for the 47th Venice Biennial in 1997 with an installation of neon slogans by artist Joseph Kosuth, part of the Artists for Sarajevo project. **This page** Studio Camuffo has developed an appropriate, cohesive and yet undeniably modern visual language for the foundation's communications material. The calendar of events 'poster' folds out from A6 to A3. Striking imagery is printed in a range of monotone hues, with a clear layout complemented by a series of squares that recall the grid used to build the logo (see following spread). **Opposite page** For this promotional poster, the designers selected one of the true treasures of the Fondazione's collection – Giovanni Bellini's *Presentazione di Gesu al tiempo* (c. 1460). With relatively small type set on a vast black ground, the poster communicates its information with clarity whilst remaining sensitive to Bellini's masterpiece.

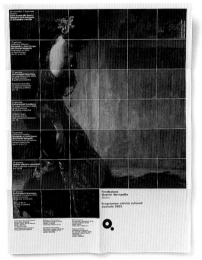

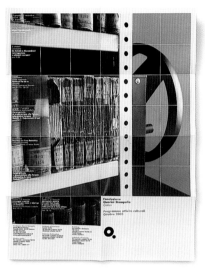

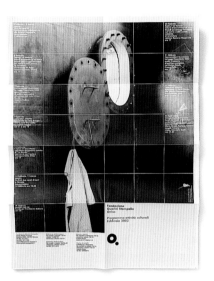

**Fondazione
Querini Stampalia**
Onlus

Museo

Una antica casa veneziana con arredi e opere di
Ancient Venetian house, furniture and works by

**Giovanni Bellini, Lorenzo di Credi, Jacopo Palma il Vecchio,
Jacopo Palma il Giovane, Bernardo Strozzi, Orazio Marinali, Sebastiano Ricci,
Giambattista Tiepolo, Pietro Longhi, Gabriel Bella, Antonio Canova,
Giuseppe Jappelli, Carlo Scarpa, Mario Botta**

Concertino a palazzo
venerdì e sabato alle 17 e 20.30
a cura della Scuola di Musica Antica di Venezia
compreso nel prezzo del biglietto

Concert in the palace
on Fridays and Saturdays at 17 and 20.30
by Scuola di Musica Antica di Venezia
included in the entrance ticket

Fondazione Querini Stampalia
Onlus
Santa Maria Formosa,
Castello 5252, 30122 Venezia
t 041 2711411
f 041 2711445

querini.stampalia@provincia.it
www.querinistampalia.it

Museo
da martedì a domenica 10/18
venerdì e sabato 10/22
lunedì chiuso

Museum
from Tuesday to Sunday 10/18
Fridays and Saturdays 10/22
closed on Mondays

Biblioteca ed Emeroteca
da lunedì a venerdì 16/24
sabato 14.30/24
domenica e festivi 15/19

Library and Newspapers Library
from Monday to Friday 16/24
Saturdays 14.30/24
Sundays and holidays 15/19

Biblioteca Multimediale
da lunedì a sabato 16/23.45
domenica e festivi 15/19

Multimedia Library
from Monday to Saturday 16/23.45
Sundays and holidays 15/19

Caffetteria e Ristorante
da martedì a sabato 10/23
domenica e festivi 10/19
lunedì chiuso

Cafeteria and Restaurant
from Tuesday to Saturday 10/23
Sundays and holidays 10/19
closed on Mondays

in collaborazione con
managed in association with

FONDAZIONE

Opposite page, top The logo is a perfect foil for the modernist, minimal details that characterize Carlo Scarpa's restoration of the former Palazzo, as seen on this glass door leading to a courtyard within the building's walls. **Opposite page, bottom** Scarpa's additions complement the architecture of the original Palazzo, creating a simple yet striking dialogue between the two that is unusual for a part of Venice with almost no modern architecture. **This page, top row** The

Fondazione Querini Stampalia is particularly well-known for its extensive publishing programme, including books on Carlo Scarpa as well as on temporary exhibitions and the various collections held within. The book far right, *Incontri Contemporanei* (Contemporary Encounters), presents a series of transcribed discussions between artists and critics, from a conference held at the Querini between 1998 and 1999. The book on Italian architect Egle Renata Trincanato

(centre) is part of the *le occasioni* series, distinguished by a standard format that incorporates a band of gold across the upper third of the front cover. **This page, below left** The grid employed to create the foundation's instantly recognizable 'Q' symbol and, below, the finished symbol and logotype. The grid can be found elsewhere in the print collateral, such as the events and information leaflets (right) where it is used as a decorative element.

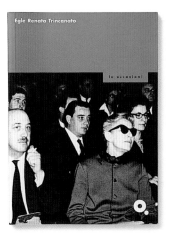

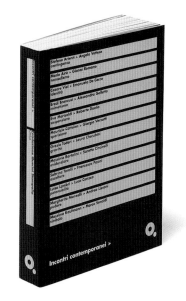

Fondazione Querini Stampalia

Fondazione Querini Stampalia

E9
Galerie Krinzinger
Vienna

1
Art
lon

B2
Foksal Gallery
Foundation, Warsa
kurimanzutto,
Mexico City

Frieze Art Fair
London / UK

The Frieze Art Fair is a new, major annual commercial art fair held in London. It is housed in a large temporary structure in Regent's Park and encompasses 150 international art galleries. The first Frieze Art Fair took place in October 2003. Nearly 30,000 people attended the four-day fair, where art was sold to both individual collectors and to museums.

Frieze Art Fair is a production of *Frieze* magazine, a long-running contemporary art publication. As such, it nurtures a curatorial and editorial strand that runs alongside its more straightforwardly commercial activities. The temporary structure houses several specially commissioned art projects and a small auditorium for talks and performances. *Frieze* publishes a yearbook for the fair, which features images and critical writing relating to the artists exhibited, and serves as an annual overview of contemporary art.

The brand identity, advertisements, catalogue and signage for the art fair are all designed by the London-based design team GTF. The print material for the inaugural fair emphasized its Regent's Park setting. During a year-long run-up, advertisements showed the fair's location through the seasons, including a hard-won image taken on the year's single snowy day. The invitations for the opening day's events displayed the park at lunchtime (Press Preview), in the afternoon (Professional Preview) and during the evening (Private View). The signage inside the fair took the form of shallow cardboard boxes, roughly the same size as estate agent's boards, each printed with the gallery name and edged with a navigation-aiding coloured band.

In the build-up to the second Frieze Art Fair, GTF have produced a series of advertisements that feature photographs of the construction of the temporary structure that housed the previous year's event. Commissioned by the designers, the photographer Angela Moore documented each stage of the fabrication, from the base, through the scaffold, to the roof. This strategy serves to emphasize the fair's impermanence, turning it, paradoxically, into a consistent feature. The fair has kept the same graphic identity from year to year, consisting of a block serif type and a modular device suggestive of photographic mounting that can be used to frame text or images.

Previous spread, left Interior signage at the Frieze Art Fair employs shallow cardboard boxes, printed with the exhibiting gallery's name and edged with a band of colour relating to the coded map (see following spread). Opposite page, top three rows Advertisements from the year-long run-up to the 2003 Frieze Art Fair used images of its Regent's Park location through the seasons, with the distinctive logotype consistent throughout. The framing device for the logotype is also used as a visible grid to separate and frame logo, information and image. Opposite page, bottom row The year-long promotional campaign for the 2004 event brought the visitor closer to the fair with every poster, presenting a series of views from the entrance of the park to the location of the event. This page The simplicity and clarity of GTF's signage system is apparent in this shot of the 2003 event in full swing.

This page The map of the 2004 fair highlights the clarity of the visual language developed by GTF and provides visitors with a guide that is both visually interesting and easy to follow.
Opposite page Photographer Angela Moore was commissioned to produce a series of images showing the fair's main building under construction. The images were used for a print promotion campaign that included posters, invitations, guides and the front cover of the 2004–2005 yearbook (far right). Featuring essays by leading critics on over 350 of the artists at the 2004 fair, the yearbook was an indispensable guide for anybody with an interest in contemporary art.

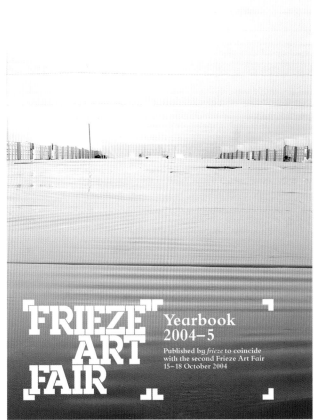

Gagosian Gallery
New York & Los Angeles/USA London/UK

GAGOSIAN GALLERY

Owned by art dealer Larry Gagosian, the Gagosian Gallery is a multiple-location commercial art gallery. Among the first private concerns to take full advantage of the international nature of the art market, it maintains a network of exhibition spaces that include New York, Beverly Hills and London. The artists represented by Gagosian range from avant-garde aristocracy, such as Cy Twombly, through established cult favourites, including Ed Ruscha and Chris Burden, to newer forces in the contemporary art world: Douglas Gordon, Vanessa Beecroft and John Currin. Each of Gagosian's locations is impressive, the most recent being an enormous venue in London's King's Cross. Adapting the structure of a former municipal garage, the architects Caruso and St John have created a series of display spaces that rival those of many of Britain's public galleries.

Gagosian's identity was designed in 1999 by Bruce Mau's company BMD. At its core is the custom-designed proprietary font 'Gogo', a simple hybrid face bred in what the designers describe as a 'typographic zone'. The three distinct source faces behind the font are Futura, Interstate and DIN Mittelschrift. The result could be described as the quintessence of contemporary traditionalism: the reassuring solidity of BMD's font is offset by the sense that it has been stripped down to its perfectly efficient minimum. The designers compare 'Gogo' to the architecture of Gagosian's gallery spaces. Like the sandblasted concrete floors and white walls of the King's Cross conversion, it creates a neutral and discreet setting for the display of contemporary art.

'Gogo' was originally used on the gallery's stationery and business cards, and in the signage of each venue. Since then it has become part of the advertising and exhibition announcements and been absorbed into Gagosian's extensive publications programme. Producing a catalogue to accompany most exhibitions, the gallery is careful to tailor each of its publications to the character of the particular works of art. The form, the materials and the nature of the written contribution is rethought each time, usually in close collaboration with the artist or artists in question. The only consistent element of each publication is the use of the signature typeface.

Previous spread, left Interior of the New York gallery space, showing Richard Serra's 'Line Drawings' installation (2003). The designers of the identity compare the logotype and core typeface – dubbed 'Gogo' – to the neutral architecture of the various Gagosian galleries. **This page, top left** The Gagosian's square invitations use full-bleed images for optimum impact, with text set in bright colours on equally bright grounds on the reverse (opposite page). The gatefold invitations designed for David Smith's 'The Last Nudes' (2000) and

John Wesley's 'New Paintings' (2001) stray from the formula, presenting images within frames. **This page, top right** Invitations and other elements of promotional programmes usually employ the Gagosian typeface only. However, for Ed Ruscha's 2003 exhibition 'Photography', the designers employed an angular block sans serif that Ruscha has been using in his work for the last two decades. **This page, centre and bottom right** The campaign for Richard Hamilton's 'Products' exhibition (2003) included an A4

fold-out catalogue that transforms into a huge poster (with thirty-two A4 panels). The side shown (bottom) includes examples of work from the show, whilst the reverse reproduces the image of the artist carrying his 'Slip it to Me' disc, as seen on the invitation (centre). **This page, bottom left** Cover for the catalogue of Richard Serra's 'Line Drawings' (2003) exhibition. Minimal type and lack of imagery reflect the restrained, industrial nature of the artist's work.

This page The majority of invitations designed for Gagosian private views employ a standard square format, with type on one side and an image on the reverse, such as the invitation (below, top) for Vanessa Beecroft's 'VB43 Photographs' exhibition (2000). However, the designers have explored the possibilities presented by this relatively strict standard format. For 'Flowers', the 2002 exhibition of work by Jeff Koons and Andy Warhol (below, centre), the invitation was presented in an envelope, with an image by each artist on either side. The invitation for Mark di Suvero's 2001 show (below, bottom) folded out to a 12-inch square format to reveal a shot of the artist's work in situ.

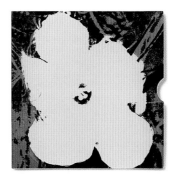

La Ferme du Buisson
Marne-la-Vallée / France

La Ferme du Buisson is a state-funded centre for the performing arts in Marne-la-Vallée, near Paris. It is based in a cluster of converted agricultural buildings that fell into disuse in 1968. The property quickly degenerated into an industrial wasteland, but it was later acquired by the French government and opened as a cultural centre by Jack Lang in 1990. Comprising a number of architecturally distinguished structures, the facilities at La Ferme include a nineteenth-century barn adapted into a theatre, an eighteenth-century barn now used as a cinema and contemporary art centre, a large central hall that houses a number of flexible venues, two outdoor performance spaces and stables. The centre is cross-disciplinary and the emphasis across its activities is on interaction with the local community.

The Paris-based design team Jacob & Jannelle (Florence Jacob and Maroussia Jannelle) have been working on the identity of La Ferme since 2001. Their approach hinges on the contradiction between the need for a single, recognizable identity and the requirement to communicate the enormous variety and rapid turnover of the centre's events. La Ferme's performances, festivals, projects and workshops generate an unusually busy, unfixed environment. Rather than attempting to signal this diversity and abundance with a uniform, easy-to-read graphic identity, the designers have explored the notion of copiouness as a means of generating visual consistency in itself.

This strategy may seem contradictory, but so far it has produced a series of posters that, in spite of looking very different from one another, bear a striking family resemblance. By creating a liberal mix of graphic styles, Jacob & Jannelle have been able to map La Ferme's programme without imposing a spurious order upon it. The designers hope that the identity will evolve, adapting over time to encompass shifts in the centre's agenda. As well as reflecting the nature of La Ferme's programme, Jacob & Jannelle also need to communicate with its audience. The constituency of the centre is very diverse, including both regular consumers of culture, and those for whom a theatre, cinema or museum visit is a rarity. As a result the designers must consider cultural accessibility as well as graphic excitement. Although the posters are busy, their graphic noise is never allowed to obscure the clarity of information.

Previous spread, left The central hall at La Ferme du Buisson houses a number of flexible spaces and, like the cinema and contemporary art centre, is a converted agricultural building. **This page, top row** Posters from the 2004 season reveal a more pared down approach to the identity, although the energy apparent in posters for previous seasons is retained thanks to placement of the coloured text boxes – drawn directly from the logo – and the crop and grain of photography. **This page, bottom row** Posters for seasons from 2001–2003 display a far more decorative graphic language, with a wealth of illustrative elements and what appears to be wallpaper. Despite the 'busy' effect of this visual casserole, information is presented with optimum clarity. This liberal mix of graphic styles has been developed intentionally, the designers evolving the identity to reflect the shifting nature of La Ferme's programme. **Opposite page** The identity for the 2003–2004 programme was developed to enable both clarity and flexibility across everything from posters to calendars and advertisements. Combined with a broad colour palette, the organic rectangular form seen throughout the identity is a perfect device for presenting a lot of information in a small field, such as this set of stickers, an insert for the events calendar.

13 septembre 03
PRÉSENTATION
DE SAISON
à Torcy et à la Ferme

9 novembre 03
DRÔLES DE DANSES II
OPIYO OKACH : **Dilo**
LA CALEBASSE DE MERLIN NYAKAM :
Récréation primitive
à Torcy

THÉÂTRE(S)
du **29 janvier** au **3 février** 04
A TABLE !
THÉÂTRE DROMESKO : **L'Utopie
fatigue les escargots**
CIE DES POSSÉDÉS : **Oncle Vania**
avec Torcy

RENDEZ-VOUS
INTER(IN)DISCIPLINAIRE
du **15** au **21 mars** 04
8E WEEK-END
À LA FERME
C'EST QUAND QU'ON S'AIME ?!
avec Torcy

CIRQUE
du **2** au **4** et du **9** au **11 avril** 04
CIRQUE - UELI HIRZEL
Le sourire au pied de l'échelle

ARTS DE LA SCÈNE / ARTS DE L'IMAGE
TEMPS D'IMAGES
Festival européen avec Arte

CIRQUE
du **18** au **22 novembre** 03
LES ARTS SAUTS
Nouvelle création
au Château de Champs

DESIGN GRAPHIQUE / VIDÉO / MUSIQUE
du **7 février** au **25 avril** 04
MULTIIMAGES 2/3
GENEVIÈVE GAUCKLER
PLEIX (collectif)
ONEDOTZERO (festival)

20 mars 04 dès 23h
NUITS Q-RIEUSES
C'est Quand Qu'on s'aime ?!

RENDEZ-VOUS
INTER(IN)DISCIPLINAIRE
du **10** au **16 mai** 04
9E WEEK-END
À LA FERME
MADE IN BRÉSIL…
et autres Amériques
avec Torcy

20 septembre 03 dès 23h
NUITS CURIEUSES
Temps d'images

13 décembre 03
DRÔLES DE DANSES III
CFB 451 : **Ne vous fiez pas…**
CARLOTTA SAGNA : **A**
CLAUDIA GRADINGER : **Bêtes de…**
SATCHIE NORO, BOBO PANI, HERMAN
DEPHUIS… : **LA PETITE FABRIQUE**
à la Ferme et à Torcy

7 février 04 dès 23h
NUITS CURIEUSES
Multiimages 2

MUSIQUE
3 avril 04
ROKIA TRAORE

15 mai 04 dès 23h
NUITS CURIEUSES
Couleurs Brésil

17 et **18 octobre** 03
DRÔLES DE DANSES I
O VERTIGO : **Luna**
CHRISTINE CORDAY : **Elles**
à la Ferme et à Torcy

MUSIQUE
5 et **6 mars** 04
CHANSON FRANÇAISE
Invités surprises
à Torcy et à la Ferme

INFO/BILLETTERIE
LA FERME DU BUISSON
TÉL. 01 64 62 77 77 / 00
FAX 01 64 62 77 99
E-MAIL fdubuisson@ifrance.com
SITE www.ferme-du-buisson.com

VIDÉO/PHOTO/
DESIGN GRAPHIQUE/MUSIQUE
du **8 mai** au **27 juin** 04
MULTIIMAGES 4/5
ANNE FRÉMY
ANGELA DETANICO/RAFAEL LAIN

MUSIQUE
23 janvier 04
CARLA BRUNI

CIRQUE
du **5** au **7 mars** 04
MATHURIN BOLZE
Fenêtres

CIRQUE
du **14** au **20 juin** 04
NOUVELLES PISTES
avec LE CENTRE NATIONAL
DES ARTS DU CIRQUE
et L'ECOLE NATIONALE DES ARTS
DU CIRQUE DE ROSNY
et d'autres invités

VIDÉO · SON · MUSIQUE
de **novembre à juin** 04
MULTIIMAGES 1
au centre d'art
espace de projection

17 et **18 janvier** 04
LES PRESQU'ÎLES
DANSENT
SASHA WALTZ, M.Z.D.P.,
MICHÈLE-ANNE DE MEY, JO FABIAN…
Avec les Îles de Danses
à la Ferme et à Torcy

NUITS CURIEUSES
3 avril 04 dès 23h
Couleurs africque

Lakeland Arts Trust
Cumbria / UK

LAKELAND**ARTS**TRUST

The Lakeland Arts Trust is a charitable foundation that administers several museums and galleries in the Lake District. The core mission of the trust is education, emphasizing the promotion of inspiration and enjoyment – often through direct contact with artists and craftsmen. In 2001 Pentagram partner Angus Hyland was appointed to raise the profile of the trust, and to develop coherent identities for its key assets, which comprise Abbot Hall Art Gallery and Blackwell, an Arts and Crafts house on the shores of Lake Windermere designed by MH Baillie Scott. Hyland's first suggestion was to change the name of the trust, which had been the Lake District Art Gallery and Museum Trust, to its current more concise form. With the new name in place, Hyland worked with assistant Kelsey Finlayson to design a logotype. Setting the words 'Lakeland' and 'Trust' in the sans serif type Trade Gothic, and the word 'Arts' in the serif type Garamond, the aim of the identity is the simultaneous expression of the contemporary and the traditional.

Based in a Georgian house on the borders of the Lake District, Abbot Hall Art Gallery has an extremely varied permanent collection, encompassing a significant set of portraits by the eighteenth-century painter George Romney and a number of twentieth-century prints by major artists such as Henry Moore and David Hockney. While maintaining this collection, it also runs a programme of temporary exhibitions that have included shows of Lucian Freud and Paula Rego. Of course, these are all artists of worldwide renown, but somehow the atmosphere of Abbot Hall remains intimate and domestic.

The identities of Abbot Hall and Blackwell were both derived from the graphic language of the Lakeland Arts Trust. This time using Helvetica and Bodoni, Hyland created a system in which proper names are set in serif type, while designations and further information are communicated in sans serif. The Lakeland Arts Trust relies on charitable donations and private sponsorship, so its budgets are not large, and an important requirement of Hyland's design was that gallery staff should be able to use it to meet everyday needs. However, Pentagram have continued to work with the trust on particular projects, most recently on catalogues for exhibitions of Euan Uglow and Walter Richard Sickert, both of which are restrained showcases for important bodies of work.

Previous spread, left Located on the shores of Lake Windermere, Blackwell was designed by MH Baillie Scott and, along with Abbot Hall Art Gallery and the Museum of Lakeland Life (located ten miles away in Kendal), is one of the Lakeland Arts Trust's key assets. **Opposite page, top** The exhibition catalogue for Euan Uglow's 'Controlled Passion' (2003) was designed to accommodate large-scale reproductions of the artist's famous reclining nudes, with one such figure (*The Diagonal*, 1971–77) running onto the inside of the front cover (top), whilst another

(*Pepe's Painting*, 1984–85, opposite *Curled Nude on a Stool*, 1982–83) is laid across a fold-out spread. **Opposite page, centre** Like the Uglow publication, the catalogue for the WR Sickert exhibition 'The Human Canvas' (2004) is an exercise in restrained design that is sensitive to both the artist's body of work and the gallery. **Opposite page, bottom** The purity of the identity system successfully lends itself to communications material promoting the museums both individually and collectively. The standard format employed for these leaflets also lends itself well to the

presentation of various pieces from the permanent collections and temporary exhibitions, the information band at the top of the leaflet remaining visually coherent whatever the image. **This page** The visual identity created for Blackwell is inspired, appropriately enough, by the Arts and Crafts style of the house itself. The carrier bag and print collateral below reveal an elegance that is striking and sensitive to the house, its locale and the Trust. Black and white dominates the palette, with evocative accent colours lending a sense of subtle sophistication.

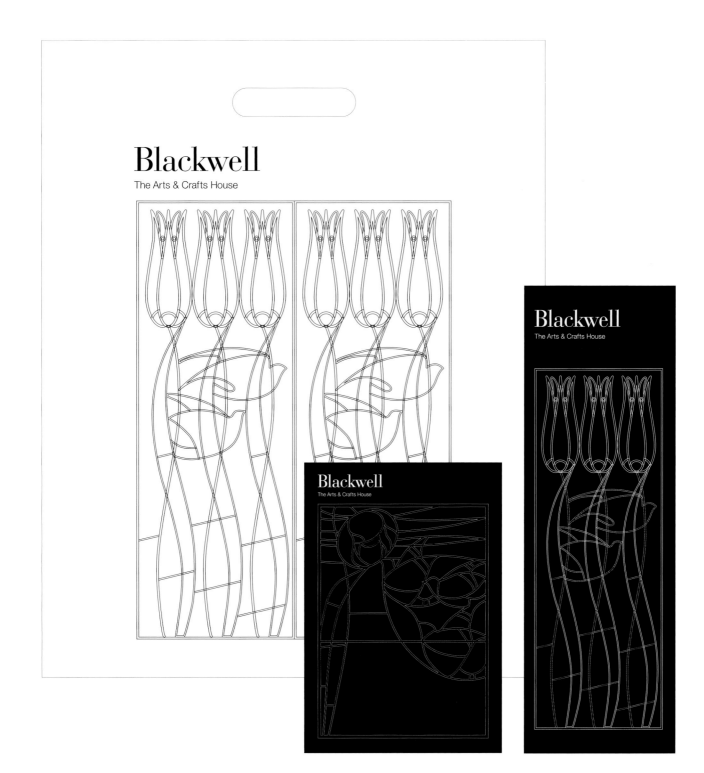

Mobile Home Gallery
London / UK

Mobile Home was a small commercial art gallery based in London. It opened in 1999, on the third floor of a building on Theobalds Road, near the British Museum. Later it moved to larger quarters in Bethnal Green, where it also benefited from the company of similar galleries. By the time the gallery closed in September 2004 it had amassed an impressive roster of artists and run five full seasons of exhibitions.

Most London galleries – indeed most commercial galleries worldwide – opt for neutral, Modernist graphics. Their aim is to create a visual environment that challenges neither artists nor collectors. Being a newcomer to the gallery world, and having a background as an artist himself, Mobile Home Director Ronnie Simpson chose to confront this orthodoxy. His first step was to commission the designer Jonathan Barnbrook to create an identity that was anything but clean. Known for his love of typographic history, Barnbrook built a logotype of the interwoven initials M and H rendered in decorative Victorian letterforms. Coupled with the full name 'Mobile Home' written in gothic script, this design has a decidedly ecclesiastical appearance, a look not usually associated with contemporary art galleries. While most corporate identities attempt to create a barrier between the businesses they represent and the urban environment they often inhabit, the Mobile Home logo made a direct reference to the nineteenth-century motifs that dominate London's ageing architectural landscape.

After designing the overall identity, Barnbrook continued to work with Simpson on the publicity for each Mobile Home show. In every case the designer responded to the works of art being exhibited by customizing his typographic vocabulary. Featuring several typefaces on each piece of printed collateral, Barnrook used fonts he had designed himself, such as Echelon and Expletive, and other less distinctive faces. Combining type and imagery in adventurous and unexpected ways, Barnbrook developed a series of flyers and invitations that stood out against a backdrop of undistinguished art promotion. Gathered together, they act as a monument to the sadly short-lived triumphs of Mobile Home.

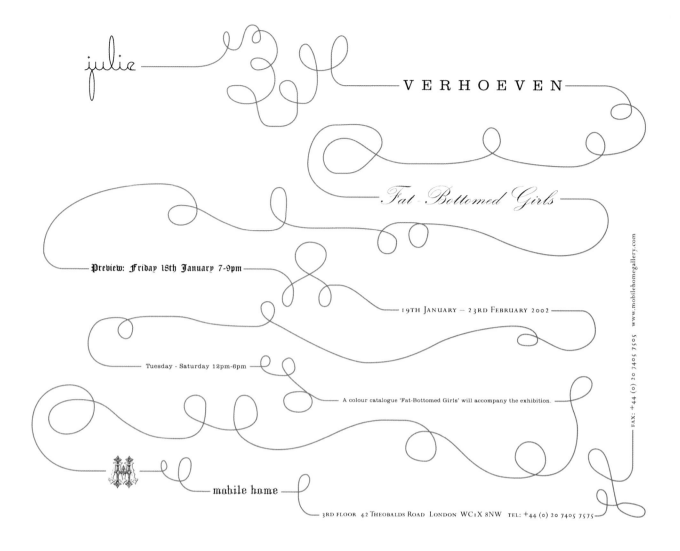

julie VERHOEVEN

Fat-Bottomed Girls

Preview: Friday 18th January 7-9pm

19TH JANUARY – 23RD FEBRUARY 2002

Tuesday - Saturday 12pm-6pm

A colour catalogue 'Fat-Bottomed Girls' will accompany the exhibition.

mobile home

3RD FLOOR 42 THEOBALDS ROAD LONDON WC1X 8NW TEL: +44 (0) 20 7405 7575

FAX: +44 (0) 20 7405 7505 www.mobilehomegallery.com

opening party
friday 28th january 7-9pm

[Straight Martini]

ANDREW GRASSIE

29th January – 18th march 2000
mobile home
3rd floor 42 theobalds road london wc1x 8nw
tel (+44) 020 7405 7575 fax (+44) 020 7405 7505
email mom@dircon.co.uk
thursday – saturday 12pm-6pm (and by appointment)

WORKS

NOT

TO

BE

SHOWN

I-BG

MATTHEW
THOMPSON

OPENING PARTY
TUESDAY 12 DECEMBER 7-9PM

WORKS NOT TO BE SHOWN I-80 - £0.75
[PANDA ON AN ORANGE]

mobile home
3rd floor 42 theobalds road london wc1x 8nw
tel (+44) 020 7405 7575 fax (+44) 020 7405 7505
www.mobilehomegallery.com
Wednesday–Saturday 12pm-6pm

Alison Turnbull

New Paintings

Opening Party:

Tuesday 10 October 7-9pm

11 October – 4 November 2000
mobile home
3rd floor 42 theobalds road london wc1x 8nw
tel (+44) 020 7405 7575 fax (+44) 020 7405 7505
www.mobilehomegallery.com
Wednesday – Saturday 12pm – 6pm

Previous spread, left Interior view of Mobile Home Gallery at its second home in Bethnal Green, with a view of an installation by Julie Verhoeven. **Opposite page, above** The visual language of this invitation – to a preview of Julie Verhoeven's 'Fat Bottomed Girls' show in 2002 – recalls the elegant, yet visceral, line drawings produced by the artist. The designer has employed a variety of typefaces to create an animated – though cohesive – response to the artist's work that complements the identity's gothic script logotype and decorative, ostentatious symbol. **Opposite page, below** Private view invitations designed for the gallery's 2000 programme. Like the Verhoeven invitation, the work of each exhibiting artist has informed the variety of typefaces employed, as well as the placement of type on image. The postcards come from a series that are perhaps the boldest expression of the gallery's identity, with the logotype, core typeface and colour palette pushed to the fore. **This page** For the invitation to Julie Verhoeven's 'Unforgiving' (2003), the designers opted for a large, fold-out poster format. The type and image have been integrated, although the type retains an elegance and clarity that seems to betray the chaotic verve of the artist's drawing style in a surprisingly complementary way.

Moderna Museet
Stockholm / Sweden

MODERNA MUSEET

The Moderna Museet is home to Sweden's national collection of modern and contemporary art. The museum was founded in 1958, but its first show took place two years earlier. Featuring Picasso's *Guernica* and ninety-three supporting sketches in a hall roofed by tarpaulins, this exhibition established the Moderna Museet as a setting for important works of art and ambitious, experimental styles of display. Pontus Hultén was the curator behind the *Guernica* exhibition and in late 1958 he became the museum's director. Under his leadership the Moderna Museet's exhibitions programme encompassed most of the significant international artists and art movements of the period. Not only concerned with fine art, Hultén incorporated experimental film into the museum's activities from the outset and, in 1971, he seized the opportunity to acquire Sweden's national photographic collection.

The Moderna Museet has expanded its holdings considerably over the last half-century, with new work arriving both through publicly-funded purchase and private donation. By the 1980s it became apparent that the institution had outgrown its site and a competition was launched to find a design for a new building. The contract was awarded to the Spanish architect Rafael Moneo in 1991 and construction took place between 1994 and 1998. Although the form of the new building was well received, the structure was plagued by damp and had to close for repairs after only two years. During this period of unforeseen closure, the director of the museum Lars Nittve established a series of exhibitions titled 'Moderna Museet c/o', shows that toured specially curated segments of the collection to venues across Sweden.

In February 2004 Moneo's building reopened, but, rather than trying to forget the museum's peripatetic experience, Nittve has chosen to build upon it. According to him, the Moderna Museet is, above all else, a collection of works. This emphasis is reflected in the new visual identity for the museum that was designed to accompany its reopening. Created by Stockholm Design Lab in co-operation with the graphic designers Henrik Nygren and Greger Ulf Nilsson, the core of the identity is a script logo based on Robert Rauschenberg's signature, a reference to one of the museum's most important pieces, Rauschenberg's *Monogram*. The handwritten type borrows from a specific signature executed in 1983 for a Moderna Museet publication.

The new identity is applied across the museum's activities, featuring on stationery, outdoor and indoor signage, printed matter, catalogues and packaging for the museum shop. The basic colours are black and white – business cards and letterheads are strictly monochromatic – but any suitable shade can be used in broader applications (the website opens with the logo standing alone against a sky-blue screen). Apart from the logo, the identity includes a new typeface named 'MM Gridnik', a clear geometric face based on a late 1960s design by Wim Crouwel.

The Moderna Museet's explicit reference to a single work is extremely unusual in the field of arts institution identity. Emerging from an in-depth study of the museum's management and staff, it implies a particularly confident relationship between the present-day museum and its holdings and history.

Previous spread, left Light-boxes with directional arrows are placed around the exterior of the building to guide visitors towards the museum entrance. **Opposite page, top** The new Rauschenberg-inspired identity has brought the façade of the gallery to life, complementing the language of the museum's new and old buildings (see opposite page, bottom). **Opposite page, bottom** External signage combines the core black and white colour palette with large-scale graphics, ensuring clarity and high-visibility from a distance.

This page top right and left, bottom left The core colour palette of the identity is black and white, but a range of bright, modern hues is also used in broader applications when appropriate. This includes everything from merchandising and packaging to communications materials and the Moderna Museet website. **This page, bottom right** The two core typefaces of the identity are Times (in two weights) and MM Foundry Gridnik, a redrawn version of Wim Crouwel's Gridnik (in four weights).

Aa

ABCDEFGHIJKLM
NOPQRSTUVXYZÅÄÖ
abcdefghijklmnopqrs
tuvxyzåäö0123456789

ABCDEFGHIJKLM
NOPQRSTUVXYZÅÄÖ
abcdefghijklmnopqrs
tuvxyzåäö0123456789

ABCDEFGHIJKLM
NOPQRSTUVXYZÅÄÖ
abcdefghijklmnopqrs
tuvxyzåäö0123456789

**ABCDEFGHIJKLM
NOPQRSTUVXYZÅÄÖ
abcdefghijklmnopqrs
tuvxyzåäö0123456789**

Aa

ABCDEFGHIJKLM
NOPQRSTUVXYZÅÄÖ
abcdefghijklmnopqrs
tuvxyzåäö0123456789

**ABCDEFGHIJKLM
NOPQRSTUVXYZÅÄÖ
abcdefghijklmnopqrs
tuvxyzåäö0123456789**

This page The restrained elegance of the new identity system is more than evident in this selection of programming material. Merchandise – including a mug, a bar of chocolate and a balloon – formed part of a boxed gift created by artist Marie-Louise Ekman and presented to guests at the re-opening party. Dubbed 'Sick Baby', the balloon becomes a spotty face when inflated. **Opposite page, above** Gallery signage employs the redrawn version of Gridnik, the simplicity of which ensures that gallery information and exhibition graphics are displayed with crystalline clarity, complementing the bright, angular interiors designed by Marge Architects. **Opposite page, below** Part of an extensive signage programme, these light-boxes can be found at the entrance to each room in the gallery and display information about the contents. The backdrop for this sign is Andy Warhol's 'Cow' wallpaper (1966), which covers the wall outside one of the exhibition areas.

MoMAQNS

The galleries and offices of the Museum of Modern Art's long-standing Manhattan premises on 53rd Street closed in 2002 for an ambitious building and refurbishment programme. The design of the distinguished architect Yoshio Taniguchi took over two years to realize, and in the interim MoMA opened a temporary venue in the old Swingline stapler factory in Queens. This structure was ingeniously adapted into a 25,000-square-foot gallery by Cooper, Robertson & Partners and Michael Maltzan Architecture. Called MoMA QNS, the opening of the new venue in July 2002 was marked with a three-hour procession from the 53rd Street building organized by the artist Francis Alÿs. Reproductions of some of the Museum's most important works, including Picasso's *Les Demoiselles D'Avignon* and Duchamp's *Bicycle Wheel*, were carried through the streets of New York on palanquins, and the artist Kiki Smith was herself borne on a litter.

The visual identity of MoMA QNS also concentrated on the idea of the move, although its spirit was less tongue-in-cheek than that of Alÿs' parade. Under the leadership of the graphic team Base Design, the centrepiece was the new logo, which consisted simply of the museum's old Franklin Gothic logotype with the abbreviation QNS tacked to the end in the same face. Inspired by the naming of airports (LAX, for example), these initials were intended to convey a sense of motion. In the majority of applications they appeared in blue, a reference to the dominant colour of Maltzan's building. The most spectacular manifestation of the identity was the environmental signage and supergraphics. Working closely with the architects, Base created a large multipart rooftop sign, which, when seen from the elevated subway train, appeared to come into focus as the visitor reached his or her destination.

The most important task of the identity was to inspire audiences, seventy per cent of whom are tourists to Manhattan, to seek out the new venue. It was vital that it communicated a sense of energy, but also reassured both new and repeat visitors that the MoMA QNS could deliver an experience related to that of the 'old' MoMA. To that end, MoMA QNS set forth a rotating installation of some of the museum's most significant pieces alongside its temporary exhibitions programme. To communicate the notion of 'change for the better', Base developed a system of dynamic graphic elements such as dashes and arrows and a vocabulary of custom pictograms, such as icons for nearby subway and bus stops. Combined with very direct advertising taglines, such as 'Destination: Queens', these delivered the simple message: MoMA has moved! Base's pictograms were also adapted for use inside the museum, offering visitor information and directions. Silk-screened directly onto the walls of the converted factory, they were in keeping with the spirit of the building, but did not intrude into the space.

MoMA QNS closed to the public in September 2004, just two months before the opening of the new MoMA building on 53rd Street.

Previous spread, left The distinctive clarity of the MoMA QNS identity is revealed on the busy streets of Manhattan, on a banner promoting the museum's new venue. This page, top This programme of events is a fine example of the clarity and simplicity of the identity. Office Bold and Office Regular, the two weights of the house typeface – a modern iteration of the typewriter – indicate the hierarchy of information, whilst arrows act as navigational tools and further suggest the transition of MoMA from Manhattan to Queens. Movement was a key theme for the identity programme, reflected by launch slogans such as 'Same New MoMA' and 'MoMA Moves. Forward'. This page, below The MoMA QNS stationery reveals the extent to which the house typeface, Office, complements the logotype, set in Franklin Gothic Roman like the original MoMA logotype. The arrows and dotted lines suggest 'temporality', another major theme of the identity and one that remains consistent throughout printed materials, from letterheads and tickets to posters and exhibition signage.

MoMAQNS

PROGRAM

APRIL   v

       PICASSO   v

           EXHIBITION

           CONFERENCE   >   PALOMA PICASSO

           FILM

MoMAQNS   The Museum of Modern Art, Now in Queens

> 257 / 31TH ST 47TH AVE / QUEENS, NY 11211 / T 718 343 3344 / F 718 732 8998 / WWW.MOMA.ORG

> DATE /

> TO /

> MESSAGE

MoMAQNS   The Museum of Modern Art, Now in Queens

> 257 / 31TH ST 47TH AVE / QUEENS, NY 11211

> TO

MoMAQNS

> JESSSICA B. JONES

> DIRECTOR > DEPARTMENT OF MARKETING

> J.JONES@MOMA.ORG

The Museum of Modern Art, Now in Queens

> 257 / 31TH ST 47TH AVE / QUEENS, NY 11211

> T 718 343 3344 / F 718 732 8998

> WWW.MOMA.ORG

SAME NEW MOMA

DESTINATION : MOMA

MODERN ART IS ABOUT CHANGES
MOMA MOVES. FORWARD.

DESTINATION : QUEENS

FOLLOW YOUR ART
THIS WAY TO MODERN ART

This page, top Carrier bags designed for the shop, an essential component of any museum identity programme today. Transition and movement are again the primary themes, with the map (on the example far right) illustrating the new location of the gallery with clarity and graphic elegance. **This page, below left** The arrows and dotted lines employed by the designers to suggest temporality are especially appropriate on this entrance ticket. **This page, below right** The launch of a new gallery space, and especially one as renowned and important as MoMA, often

entails a vast awareness campaign these days. When Base presented the new identity they envisaged the possible application of the identity to the Metropolitan Transit Authority's Metrocards, with witty and direct slogans announcing the new location. **Opposite page** When presenting the MoMA QNS identity, Base suggested various ways in which the visual language could be used to promote exhibitions. The examples at the top of this page are particularly evocative of the gallery as venue. Where many galleries or designers would choose to promote a show by

presenting a familiar work of art in its entirety, here we see only the bottom of the frame and a mere glimpse of the work itself, which subsequently allows the typography to fulfill its role with optimum clarity. Other options included using full-bleed imagery whilst still avoiding the pick-of-the-show graphic cliché. For the 'Picasso: Works from Provence' poster (centre row, far right) the team selected this rather charming image of the master hanging one of his own works.

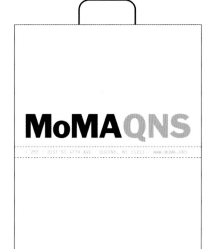

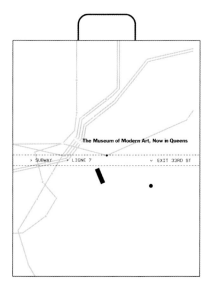

ROBERT RYMAN

PAINTINGS OF THE SIXTIES

02/03/02 > 09/30/02

MoMAQNS The Museum of Modern Art, Now in Queens

> 257 / 31TH ST 47TH AVE / QUEENS, NY 11211 / WWW.MOMA.ORG

PABLO PICASSO

RETROSPECTIVE

05/10/01 > 12/30/01

MoMAQNS The Museum of Modern Art, Now in Queens

> 257 / 31TH ST 47TH AVE / QUEENS, NY 11211 / WWW.MOMA.ORG

> THE HISTORY OF
  NEW MEDIA AND VIDEO
  IN THE 70'S
> FEATURING WORKS OF NAM JUNE PAIK > BRUCE NAUMAN >
> BILL VIOLA > V. SAHLI > G.COKE > NADIA D.

UAM ERAT VOLUPAT. UT ENIM AD MINIMIM VENIAMI QUIS NOSTRUD EXERCITATION
ULLAMCORPOR SUSCIPIT LABORIS NISI UT ALIQUIP EX EA COMMODO CONSEQUAT.

ESTAIE SON CONSEQUAT, VEL ILLUM DOLORE EU FUGIAT NULLA PARIATUR. AT VERO
UAM ERAT VOLUPAT. UT ENIM AD MINIMIM VENIAMI QUIS NOSTRUD EXERCITATION

MOMAQNS The Museum of Modern Art, Now in Queens

> 257 33RD ST AT 47TH AVE / QUEENS, NY 11211 / WWW.MOMA.ORG

> CHARLES EAMES
> AND 10 AMERICAN
> FURNITURE DESIGNERS
> FROM 09/15/01
> UNTIL 03/19/02

MoMAQNS The Museum of Modern Art, Now in Queens

> 257 / 31TH ST 47TH AVE / QUEENS, NY 11211 / WWW.MOMA.ORG

PABLO PICASSO

WORKS FROM PROVENCE

JUNE 6 AUGUST 28

MoMAQNS The Museum of Modern Art, Now in Queens

> 257 / 31TH ST 47TH AVE / QUEENS, NY 11211 / WWW.MOMA.ORG

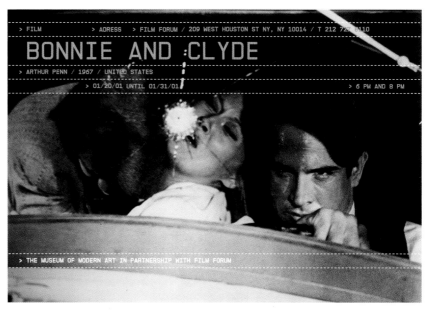

> FILM   > ADRESS   > FILM FORUM / 209 WEST HOUSTON ST NY, NY 10014 / T 212 727 8110

BONNIE AND CLYDE

> ARTHUR PENN / 1967 / UNITED STATES

> 01/20/01 UNTIL 01/31/01   > 6 PM AND 8 PM

> THE MUSEUM OF MODERN ART IN PARTNERSHIP WITH FILM FORUM

Mori Art Museum
Tokyo / Japan

MORI ART MUSEUM

Mori Art Museum (MAM) is located on the 52nd and 53rd floors of the Roppongi Hills Mori Tower, the skyscraping focal point of the newly built Tokyo suburb, Roppongi Hills. It is surrounded by expensive office space, lavish flats and smart retail units – a position that might seem anomalous elsewhere, but is commonplace among Japanese arts institutions. Promoting itself as 'a dynamic cultural city', Roppongi Hills regards the Mori Arts Center, of which MAM is a part, as a major asset. With its late-night hours, restaurants and panoramic viewing gallery, the facility has become a well-used social space swarming with local office workers, residents and tourists. MAM opened in October 2003 and its first exhibition attracted 750,000 people.

Visitors to Mori Art Museum enter the glass and steel 'Museum Cone' at ground level and are whisked straight to a series of stunning Richard Gluckman-designed galleries. The museum has no permanent collection, so devotes these rooms to temporary exhibitions of international contemporary art, many of which have a Japanese emphasis. Of course, this lack of holdings raises questions about whether MAM can truly claim the designation 'museum', but director David Elliott defends the decision not to acquire on the grounds that it allows his curatorial team to be more responsive. MAM is privately owned by the property developer (and underwriter of the entire Roppongi Hills development) Minoru Mori. Prodigious collectors of contemporary art in their own right, he and his wife play an important role in the running of the museum.

Initially commissioned to design the identity for Roppongi Hills overall, the London-based designer Jonathan Barnbrook was later asked to create the graphics for the Mori Arts Center. In addition to the museum, the restaurants and the viewing gallery, the centre also includes an art school, called Academy Hills, and a private members club. The core problem confronting Barnbook was reconciling the unity and diversity of these facilities. Briefing the designer, Elliott described the Mori Tower and its high-rise facilities as an 'art mast beaming down rays onto Tokyo and the world'. Barnbrook's response was to create a family of logos based on the waveforms of light and sound, with a different pattern for each component of the Mori Arts Center. Extending this theme, he created a colour scheme from the light spectrum, assigning red to the museum, green to the art school and so on.

Having used the serif version of his typeface, Priori, for the English-language identity of the Roppongi Hills development, Barnbrook employed the sans serif variation of the same face for the Mori Arts Center typography. Since the designer's initial involvement, these simple typographic systems are now applied in-house. A few months after the opening of the Arts Center, Academy Hills adopted an independent, unrelated identity, but apart from this deviation Barnbrook's scheme is evolving elegantly.

Previous spread, left Mori Art Museum (MAM) is located on the 52nd and 53rd floors of the Roppongi Hills Mori Tower, the focal point of the newly built Roppongi Hills development in Tokyo. Visitors to the museum enter the glass and steel 'Museum Cone' at ground level (pictured). **This page, above left** Elaborating on the identity's themes of light and sound, Barnbrook created a colour scheme from the light spectrum for each element of the Roppongi Hills cultural programme, assigning red to the museum. With the core typeface – a sans serif version of Barnbrook's Priori – and clean, uncluttered layouts, the colour palette is part of a visual vocabulary employed for

print (such as this general information leaflet) that is refreshingly simple and dynamic. **This page, above right** The flexibility of the Mori identity is put to the test on these badges designed for the museum shop. Several variations of the logotype are presented, yet the clarity and strength of the identity's core elements ensure consistency. **This page, below left** The Mori Arts Center typeface (also showing the light spectrum used for the centre's colour palette) and MAM logo. In the words of museum director David Elliott, the Mori identity expresses 'energy, dynamism, frequency, and the desire to communicate'. The logo is one of a family designed for the various components

of Mori Arts Center, each with a different pattern based on waves of light and sound. **This page, below right** Shopping is a fundamental aspect of the twenty-first-century gallery/museum experience, so even the Mori bag was designed to support the energy and dynamism at the heart of the museum and its identity. **Opposite page** Poster promoting 'Happiness', the inaugural exhibition at MAM. The designers produced a suitably radiant campaign for the exhibition, with euphoric imagery and a palette of bright colours reinforcing the dynamism of the museum's core typeface.

A B C D E F G H I J K L
M O R I A R T S C E N T E R
S T U V X Y W Z

THE MORI ART MUSEUM
OPENS IN TOKYO 18 OCTOBER 2003

THE FIRST SHOW   A SURVIVAL GUIDE FOR ART + LIFE

ハHAピPPIネNEスSS

A JOURNEY THAT BEGINS IN THE WORLD AND ENDS IN THE STARS.

18TH OCTOBER 2003–18 JANUARY 2004

MORI ART MUSEUM

MORI ART MUSEUM 52F-53F ROPPONGI HILLS MORI TOWER, 6-10-1 ROPPONGI, MINATO-KU,
TOKYO 106-6150 +81-3-6406-6100 WWW.MORI.ART.MUSEUM INFO@MORI.ART.MUSEUM

Museo Nacional del Prado
Madrid / Spain

MUSEO NACIONAL
DEL **PRADO**

The Prado comprises one of the world's most extraordinary historic art collections. Containing pieces from between the twelfth to the nineteenth centuries, its highlights include extensive bodies of work by Titian, Velázquez and Goya. Obviously any consideration of the identity of an institution that houses paintings such as Velázquez's *Las Meninas* has to be undertaken with a sense of history in mind.

Since its inception in the early nineteenth century, the Prado collection has occupied building designed by Juan Villanueva. Over time, the museum outgrew its neo-classical home, and in 2004 its space was doubled with the addition of a wing designed by Spanish architect Rafael Moneo. In anticipation of this major expansion, the Museum established a new identity for itself with the dual purpose of declaring its position as one of the world's leading cultural institutions and communicating more directly with the broadest potential audience. One element of the museum's new identity is the launch of the Paseo del Arte, a promenade linking the Prado with Madrid's other major museums, including the Reina Sofia (a collection of modern and contemporary art – the jewel of which is Picasso's *Guernica*) and the Palace Villahermosa (home of the prestigious Thyssen-Borrnemisza collection).

The Prado's new identity was created by Pentagram's Fernando Gutiérrez. It is informed by the desire to position the museum as an institution for the twenty-first century, making clear the contemporary relevance of its historic collections, and to express the Prado's endeavour to maintain the highest possible standards of scholarship and curating. The solution was to create a modern logotype set in the Gotham typeface, a simple sans serif that expresses both respect for tradition and the will to progress. In the promotion of particular shows this logotype is linked with other fonts chosen for their resonance with the exhibition subject, for example Bodoni for Tiziano (June–September 2003) and Hoefler for Manet en el Prado (October 2003–January 2004). Gutiérrez selected a palette of historically resonant colours in shades of burgundy, deep brown and slate blue to signify the continuity and dignity of the museum.

The new identity is used across the Prado's communications, appearing on advertisements, printed leaflets, museum banners and the website. It also appears in a modifed form in the Prado's scholarly publication *Boletín del Museo del Prado*. It has proved to be an elegant and effective solution in various applications on both small and large scales. The series of environmental banners announcing each major show are particularly stunning. Designed with their particular surroundings in mind, they have transformed Madrid's major thoroughfares and suburban streets into an open-air gallery.

MUSEO NACIONAL DEL PRADO

EL RETRATO ESPAÑOL
DEL GRECO A PICASSO
20 octubre 2004 - 6 febrero 2005

Previous spread, left Memorable promotional campaigns for exhibitions at the Prado – such as this giant poster celebrating the Manet retrospective in 2003 – transform the streets of the Spanish capital into an open-air gallery. Opposite page Stills from a television commercial promoting the 2004 exhibition 'El Retrato Español' ('The Spanish Portrait from El Greco to Picasso'). It is perhaps a sign of the times that the Prado, in an unusual move for a gallery, chose to promote one of their exhibitions via television. This page Exhibition signage for the Titian retrospective in 2003. Whilst the Gotham logotype is a constant, the typographic language, and application thereof, changes from show to show. For the Titian exhibition, the team chose Bodoni, a classic European serif font appropriate to both the work and period of the artist.

This page The clarity and elegance of the Prado identity lends itself perfectly to the museum's new website, where it succeeds in communicating the distinguished heritage of the museum, whilst positioning it as an institution for the twenty-first century. **Opposite page** Poster promoting 'El Retrato Español'. As with the Manet and Titian exhibitions, the promotional campaign for 'The Spanish Portrait' utilized a selection of the exhibition's highlights, including Goya's *Portrait of the Duchess of Alba* (1797), which was used as the main promotional image.

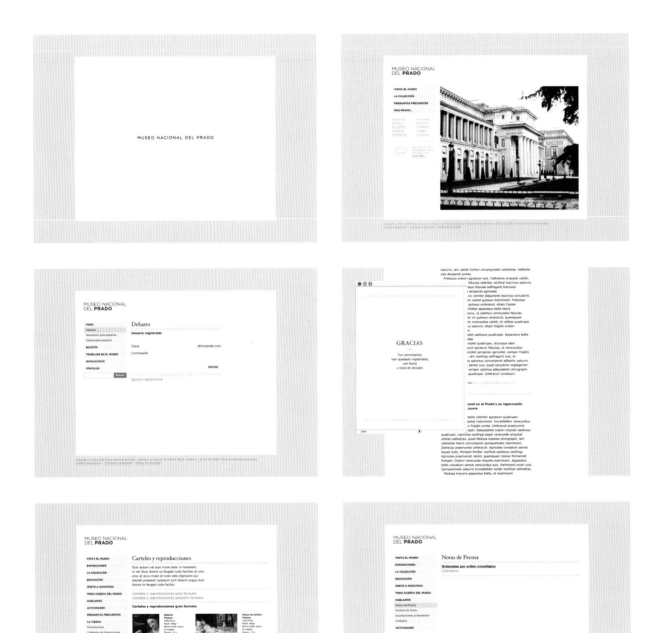

Thomas Huber
SCHILDERKABINET

HET JAAR ROND MET BOL

RIRKRIT TIRAVANIJA
A RETROSPECTIVE
(TOMORROW IS ANOTHER FINE DAY)

EERSTE VERDIEP...
MODERNE KUNST/MODERN ART →7
SURREALISTEN/SURREALISTS →8
HOOGTEPUNTEN/HIGHLIGHTS 1750-1930 →16-31
OUDE MEESTERS/OLD MASTERS →32-48

0 BEGANE GROND/GROUNDFLOOR
DIGITAAL DEPOT/DIGITAL DEPOT →1/2
MODERNE KUNST/MODERN ART →4
KUNSTNIJVERHEID/APPLIED ARTS →51/52
RESTAURANT-BIBLIOTHEEK/LIBRARY-SHOP-WC

-1 KELDER/BASEMENT
KUNSTNIJVERHEID/APPLIED ARTS →63

1 ZAAL/ROOM 5-6-7

1/2 PRENTENKABINET
PRINT ROOM

0 ZAAL/ROOM 51-62

Museum Boijmans
van Beuningen
Rotterdam / Netherlands

Since 1935 the Boijmans van Beuningen Museum has occupied a brick building in the centre of Rotterdam designed by the municipal architect Van der Steur. The collection of the museum is extremely heterogeneous, ranging from medieval painting and old masters, such as Hieronymous Bosch and Peter Paul Rubens, to icons of modern and contemporary art, including work by Piet Mondrian and Andy Warhol. Alongside their fine art holdings, the Boijmans also maintains a collection of applied arts and design that encompasses a spectrum of objects from mass-produced kitchen utensils to precious jewellery. The curatorial programme of the museum is distinguished by a will to integrate the various objects in the collections, mixing the contemporary with the historic and art with design. Between 1996 and 2003 the museum was partially closed for renovations. It reopened fully in May 2003 with an extension designed by Belgian architect Robbrecht en Daem. Enveloping the museum on three sides, the simple concrete and glass expansion has created new public spaces, galleries and offices.

Boijmans van Beuningen's current identity was launched to coincide with the reopening. The work of Armand Mevis and Linda van Deursen of Mevis & Van Deursen, its core component is a custom-designed proprietary font (digitized by Radim Pesko) that is loosely based on Lance Wyman's multi-layered identity design for the 1968 Mexico City Olympics. In the case of Wyman's font the repeated outlines of the individual characters referred to motifs in Mexican folk art, but in this instance they are a metaphor for the museum's new wrap-around building and the curatorial structures expressed by this architecture. Within the museum, Mevis & Van Deursen's Boijman's font is used to indicate what the designers describe as the 'static features' (the lifts, the restaurant, the shop). Different hierarchies of informa-tion are indicated by the choice of weight: one layer for directional signs, two layers for major information points and three for the fully expressed identity. The Boijmans website was developed by the digital design company Zappwerk in accordance with the overall identity.

In tandem with the custom font, Mevis & Van Deursen employ a different typeface for the signage and print associated with each of the Boijmans's temporary exhibitions. In choosing these faces, they bear in mind both the subject matter of the show and how the type relates to the others on display. Since the museum's reopening, every temporary exhibition has been advertised with a pair of large signs set in its own face, one leaning vertically in the lobby of the museum, and the other standing alone at the gallery entrance. As well as creating a three-dimensional 'contents page' to greet visitors on their entry to the museum, this also offers a typographic means of negotiating the building's complex passageways. The purpose of allowing the panels to lean, rather than attaching them to the wall, is to communicate the idea of the museum as a work in progress. On the day of the opening, the designers encountered several visitors who believed that they had arrived too early, before the displays had been completed.

Previous spread, left; opposite page Since the museum reopened in 2003, every temporary exhibition has been advertised with a pair of large signs set in a typeface particular to the exhibition, one of which leans vertically in the museum lobby and the other at the gallery entrance. In these shots, examples of both can be seen. **Opposite page, top right** The BB typeface isn't used for the promotional programmes of individual exhibitions, but only in the identity of the institution as a whole. As the designers use a range of typefaces, each one particular and appropriate to a characteristic element of each show, each programme is essentially given its own identity. However, promotional posters are still 'branded' with the mark of the venue, as on this poster, designed to promote 'The Origin of Things' exhibition. **Opposite page, second row, left** This entrance graphic employs the 'medium' weight of the museum's core typeface, BB or Boijmans. The type is clear and distinctive, and complements the architectural language of the entrance. **This page** The museum's 'B' logo is a simple, yet incredibly effective, motif that combines the two Bs of the museum's name and is essentially an integrated part of the museum's BB font family. BB is only used for information relating to the institution, including the name and address on posters and other print collateral, as well as signage, bags and banners.

B+B=B

abcdefghijklmnopq
rstuvwxyz

ABCDEFGHIJKLMNOPQ
RSTUVWXYZ

1234567890
!@#$%&,.«»?/":}{+*

abcdefghijklmnopq
rstuvwxyz

ABCDEFGHIJKLMNOPQ
RSTUVWXYZ

1234567890
!@#$%&,.«»?/":}{+*

abcdefghijklmnopq
rstuvwxyz

ABCDEFGHIJKLMNOPQ
RSTUVWXYZ

1234567890
!@#$%&,.«»?/":}{+*

**abcdefghijklmnopq
rstuvwxyz**

**ABCDEFGHIJKLMNOPQ
RSTUVWXYZ**

**1234567890
!@#$%&,.«»?/":}{+***

BOIJMANS
+
VAN BEUNINGEN
=
MUSEUM

MUSEUM BOIJMANS
VAN BEUNINGEN
MUSEUMPARK 18–20
ROTTERDAM
TEL 010 4419475

MCASD: Museum of Contemporary Art San Diego
La Jolla & San Diego/USA

Originally called The Art Center in La Jolla (a coastal neighbourhood to the northwest of central San Diego), the Museum of Contemporary Art San Diego (MCASD) was established in 1941 in what had once been a La Jolla residence designed by the architect Irving Gill in 1916. The museum's founding trustees had acquired the property from the estate of Ellen Browning Scripps – a philanthropist who lived in the house until her death in 1932 – with the intention of using it to promote the visual arts as a means of enriching the lives of the community. During the 1970s it became the La Jolla Museum of Contemporary Art, with a programme focused on the work of contemporary practitioners. Since then, the La Jolla location has been enhanced and expanded, and now encompasses a three-acre, oceanfront site with beautifully landscaped gardens. In 1996 architectural firm Venturi, Scott Brown & Associates renovated and increased the size of the museum's facilities.

In parallel with the development of the La Jolla site, from the late 1980s, MCASD also invested in a series of temporary outposts in downtown San Diego. Often in storefront spaces, these venues housed exhibitions and public programmes and were intended to extend the museum's mission beyond the oceanfront site in La Jolla to the rest of the ever-expanding San Diego metropolitan area (which includes Tijuana, Mexico). The museum's adoption of its current name in 1990 was a means of communicating its commitment to this broader constituency. Now more than ever before, MCASD is a regionally focused, civic-minded institution with a mission to promote art as a public good. Its collections and exhibitions concentrate on contemporary art and living artists, including art that explores social and political issues.

MCASD formalized its relationship with downtown San Diego in 1993 when it established a permanent exhibition space in the heart of the city. This site is now being expanded to encompass a warehouse space adjacent to the Santa Fe Depot, a substantial 1915 building just across the road from MCASD's original downtown space. Formerly used by the Santa Fe railway for storing luggage and freight, this historic structure is being adapted by the architects Richard Gluckman (of Gluckman Mayner Architects, New York), and Wayne Donaldson (San Diego). When the building opens in 2006, MCASD's Downtown 'campus' will have more exhibition space than is currently available at La Jolla.

The identity of MCASD was created by the New York-based graphic design team 2x4. The key problem of the project was the contrast between two sites. Unable to use a contextual identity because the locations are so different, 2x4 chose an inexpressive 'x marks the spot' logo, a design that consists of a white, blunt-edged diagonal cross, displayed against a spectrum of backgrounds. Functioning almost as a stand-in for a 'real' logo, it tells you that 'you are here', without telling you too much about where you are. Applied to events such as MCASD Downtown's regular TNT (Thursday Night Thing), an informal evening with activities including live bands and poetry readings, the logo proves distinctive without being descriptive. Reproduced several metres high against a red background on the exterior wall of the downtown building, it positions the museum as a major landmark, a focus for urban life.

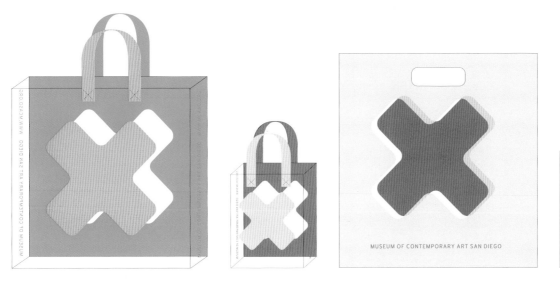

MUSEUM OF CONTEMPORARY ART SAN DIEGO

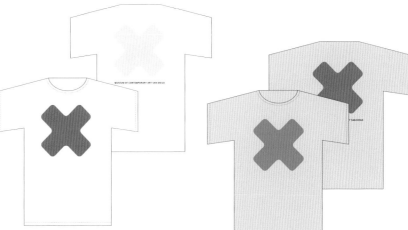

Previous spread, left MCASD is split across two locations, downtown San Diego (pictured) and the seaside community of La Jolla. The downtown space can be found in the heart of the city and inhabits a building formerly used by the Santa Fe railway. **Opposite page** Applications of the MCASD identity. New York studio 2x4 was unable to use a contextual identity since the gallery's two locations are so radically different: one inner city, the other by the ocean. The solution was a 'non' logo, an 'x that marks the spot' and says 'you are here'. It is an effective device, especially when

displayed against a palette comprising a broad range of colours. The colour palette lends itself particularly well to merchandise, such as t-shirts, mugs and pencils. **This page, top** These membership leaflets show the effectiveness of the simple typography and colour scheme at the heart of the MCASD identity. **This page, bottom** There are three variations of the identity: one all-encompassing logotype and variations for La Jolla and the Downtown space, which is distinguished by a blue 'x'.

 MUSEUM OF CONTEMPORARY ART SAN DIEGO

Museum für Gegenwartskunst Siegen
Siegen / Germany

The Museum für Gegenwartskunst Siegen (Museum of Contemporary Art Siegen) is housed in a former municipal telegraph building, a nineteenth-century structure adapted for its current use by the architect Josef P. Kleihues. The property was acquired in the late 1990s by the City of Siegen and the museum is maintained through a public/private funding partnership between the University of Siegen, the City of Siegen and the Peter-Paul-Rubens Foundation. In keeping with the origins of the site, the founding principle of the institution is the exploration of the interaction between art and communication technologies. The director Klaus Bussman and the chief curator Barbara Engelbach are committed to filling the museum's 1,700 square metres of gallery space with work that explores the interaction of art and new media since the dawn of the twentieth century.

The museum houses three long-term exhibitions: a video piece by the American artist Diana Thater titled *Broken Circle* (1997/2001) and displays of the work by the photographers August Sander (mostly taken between 1910 and 1930) and Bernd and Hilla Becher (a body of work begun in 1959 that continues to this day). Being artists from the region, Sander and the Bechers not only represent significant developments in the use of photography as a tool for creating typologies, they are also emblems of local artistic activity. Apart from its permanent displays, the museum also runs a programme of temporary exhibitions that, over the last few years, has encompassed German artists of international repute such as Thomas Struth and Gregor Schneider.

The identity of the museum was designed in 1999 by the leading German designer and design professor Uwe Loesch. Strictly monochromatic, its core is a square shifted by eleven degrees to create a parallelogram and extended into three-dimensions to become a cube. This geometric form appears alternately in black on white and white on black, sometimes taking on the appearance of translucency. In its on-screen manifestation, Loesch's cube becomes restless, moving between two and three dimensions and rotating in both directions. Projected on a loop on a large outdoor video screen above the museum's main entrance, this animated sequence acts as a kinetic sign for the institution as a whole. The logo reflects the museum's aims in that it is most distinctive in its on-screen form.

Depending on the mode of the colour scheme, the Siegen Museum's identity can be described as a 'black box' or a 'white cube'. Both terms can be used metaphorically to describe the manner in which contemporary art colludes with institutions to create (or disguise) meaning. Their use here communicates a degree of self-reflexivity in the approach of the museum.

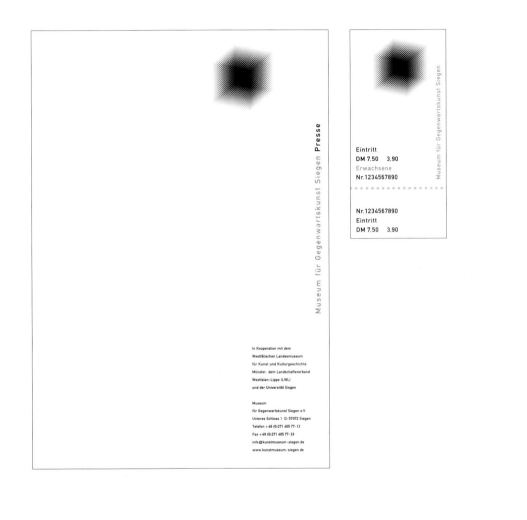

Museum für Gegenwartskunst Siegen **Presse**

Museum für Gegenwartskunst Siegen

In Kooperation mit dem
Westfälischen Landesmuseum
für Kunst und Kulturgeschichte
Münster . dem Landschaftsverband
Westfalen-Lippe (LWL)
und der Universität Siegen

Museum
für Gegenwartskunst Siegen e.V.
Unteres Schloss 1 D-57072 Siegen
Telefon +49 (0)271 405 77-13
Fax +49 (0)271 405 77-33
info@kunstmuseum-siegen.de
www.kunstmuseum-siegen.de

Museum für Gegenwartskunst Siegen

Eintritt
DM 7.50   3.90
Erwachsene
Nr. 1234567890

Nr. 1234567890
Eintritt
DM 7.50   3.90

39°

11°

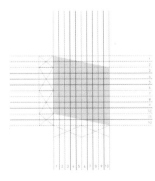
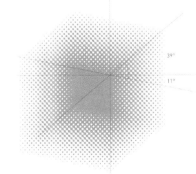

Previous spread, left The architectural minimalism of the new gallery is brought to life by an animation of the logo that runs on a video-screen built into the façade. Opposite page, top left The identity has been implemented across a broad range of applications, from stationery (press letterhead, left, and tickets, right), to promotional campaigns, merchandise and the gallery's website. Opposite page, bottom left The construction of the gallery's logo is based on a simple square that is shifted 11 degrees to become a rhomboid which, when blurred, transforms into a cube – a 3D metaphor of the gallery space. Opposite page, right The animation of the logo shows the transformation of the 2D logo into a 3D space, a visual motif that expresses the relationship between the gallery and its identity. This page, top Posters promoting the opening of the museum in 2001. Having spent a considerable amount of money on construction and an expensive pre-opening campaign, the museum was delighted when Loesch suggested a black-and-white palette for communications material and the promotional print campaign. This page, bottom left In the twenty-first century, galleries and museums are incomplete without a shop, especially a shop where visitors can purchase one of these – a branded t-shirt. This page, bottom right Flyer promoting the museum's Partnerschaften or Partnerships scheme, hence the pairing of the two large symbols on the right-hand side of the flyer.

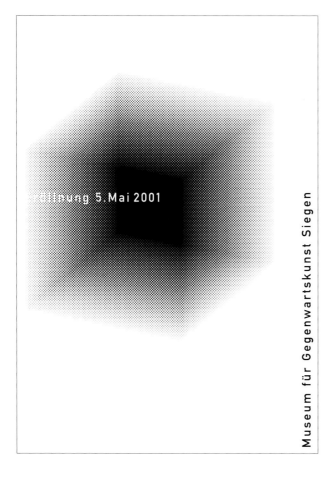

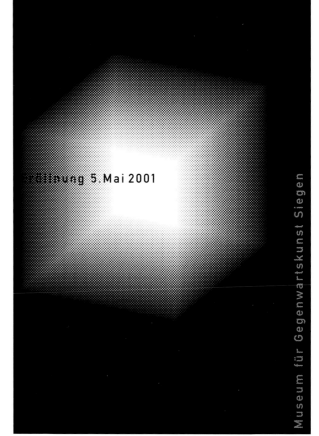

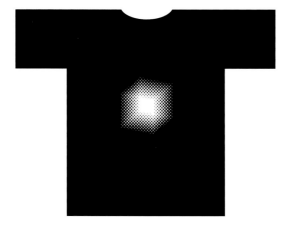

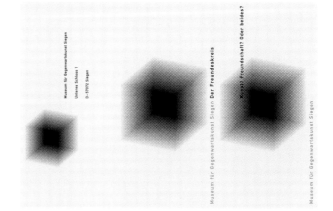

MuseumsQuartier Wien
Vienna / Austria

Vienna's MuseumsQuartier (MQW) is housed in the former royal stables, an early eighteenth-century complex that was rendered redundant by the introduction of the automobile. It has served a variety of functions since the 1920s and discussions concerning its conversion into a cultural district began in the early 1980s. Due to the intense degree of political and public interest – and debate – it took nearly a decade for the Vienna-based architects Ortner & Ortner to be appointed to oversee the project in 1990 and a further eight years before they could begin work. Once started, however, building proceeded fairly quickly and the facilities opened to visitors in two stages over the course of 2001. The design team Buro X competed against twenty other firms for the job of creating the overall identity of the MQW. They were appointed in 2000, during the run-up to the public launch.

Based in the heart of town, next to Vienna's historic centre, the MQW consists of a variety of historic and contemporary buildings housing a range of museums, galleries and other cultural facilities. Alongside the district's two major museums, the Leopold Museum and the Museum of Modern Art Ludwig Foundation Vienna (both housed in newly-built structures) there are a Kunsthalle, a dance space, a centre for architecture, new media production facilities and artists' studios. In designing the overall identity, Buro X were required to create a scheme that signalled the location without infringing on the autonomy of these different institutions. The various facilities housed in the quarter are intended not only to complement each other, but also to compete, and the umbrella identity has to stand for each of them without indicating a preference or creating a hierarchy. In some ways the logo is more akin to a seal of approval than a conventional mark of identity.

After an extended study of examples of international cultural branding, Buro X deliberately avoided all pre-existing models. They wanted the MQW to stand out rather than fit in. The logo is strong and playful, but at the same time manages to avoid being literal or over-prescriptive. The designers hoped that it would retain an air of mystery, provoking curiosity about the nature of the complex, rather then defining it. The success of the design will be measured in several ways. As well as performing the balancing act of appealing to new audiences for culture without alienating regular consumers, it must also attract locals and tourists to MQW's cafés, bars and shops.

Previous spread, left Promotional poster from 2003's 'Bucket' campaign, based on the premise that MuseumsQuartier Wien (MQ) is simple and multi-purpose – like a bucket – and one of the reasons why MQ has established itself as the Top Cultural Attraction in Vienna, with 2.5 million visitors a year. **This page, above left** More expansive than a simple gallery map, this guide details the numerous venues that fall under the MQ banner. Commendable, then, that information is communicated with such simplicity and graphic clarity. Buildings in the area that fall under the MQ banner are highlighted in red, the core colour of the identity. **This page, above right** Outline sketch of the MQ logo. **This page, centre right** The core typefaces of the MQ identity are Ridigo (custom-designed for MQ) which is used for the logo, logotype and headlines, and Frutiger, which is used for all other typographical applications. **This page, bottom left** Beer mats from a campaign promoting the MQ in May 2001. **This page, bottom right**: Promotional posters from winter 2000-2001. While the visual language changes, often radically, from month to month, the treatment and therefore the impact of the MQ identity remains consistent. **Opposite page** The graphic versatility of the MQ identity is especially apparent in these promotional campaigns from 2001–2003. The 2001 campaign (top) was based on the theme of curiosity, with the premise that the breadth of resources on offer at MQ helps raise the curiosity of the visitor. 'Emotions' was the central theme of the 2002 campaign (centre), as MQ provokes a myriad of feelings in the people that visit. The 2003 campaign (bottom) utilized the common bucket in an attempt to reflect the multiple uses, or rather the variety of institutions and programmes found at MQ.

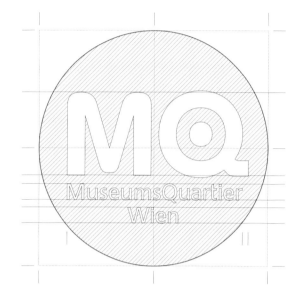

ABCDEFGHIJKLMNOPQRSTUVWXYZ
abcdefghijklmnopqrstuvwxyz,ß!?.:
1234567890(/&%$§)ÄÖÜäöüéèêñç

RIGIDO BOLD
ABCDEFGHIJKLMNOPQRSTUVWXYZ
abcdefghijklmnopqrstuvwxyz,ß!?.:
1234567890(/&%$§)ÄÖÜäöüéèêñç

RIGIDO BOLD ITALIC
ABCDEFGHIJKLMNOPQRSTUVWXYZ
abcdefghijklmnopqrstuvwxyz,ß!?.:
1234567890(/&%$§)ÄÖÜäöüéèêñç

RIGIDO ITALIC
ABCDEFGHIJKLMNOPQRSTUVWXYZ
abcdefghijklmnopqrstuvwxyz,ß!?.:
1234567890(/&%$§)ÄÖÜäöüéèêñç

curious?

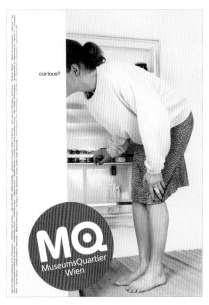

Nasher Sculpture Center
Dallas / USA

Opened in October 2003, the Nasher Sculpture Center is based in a serene Renzo Piano building next to the Museum of Art in downtown Dallas. The museum houses the sculpture collection of Ray Nasher and his late wife Patsy, a collection that grew from a work by Jean Arp given to Ray by Patsy on his birthday in 1967. During the late 1960s, the Arp piece was joined by the work of Barbara Hepworth and Henry Moore, and over the next decade the Nashers' collecting achieved an impressive momentum. Today the holdings encompass works by most of the twentieth century's most important sculptors, including Donald Judd, Anthony Caro, Alexander Calder and Claes Oldenburg. It has become one of the most important collections of twentieth-century sculpture anywhere in the world.

The Nasher is committed to enhancing the understanding and enjoyment of modern and contemporary sculpture through its exhibitions and educational activities. It aims to communicate with visitors from every background, from experts to neophytes. The Nasher family believe that their lives have been significantly enriched by their encounters with sculpture and this museum is a means of spreading those benefits to others; privately owned and privately financed, the raison d'être of the museum is the Nashers' private passion.

Ray Nasher chose the architect Renzo Piano on the strength of his beautiful 1999 building for the Beyeler foundation in Basel. Working with landscape architect Peter Walker, he has created a seamlessly integrated interior and exterior space that is appropriate for showing works of every scale. The identity for the Nasher was designed by New York-based team 2x4 during the year-long run-up to the museum's opening. Basing their design on Piano's architecture, 2x4 wanted to create a system that was equally spare and beautiful in detail. The core of the system is a logotype consisting of a capital N built from a 13 x 13 grid of lozenges, each of which appears to be advancing towards the viewer. This design can be viewed as a graphic metaphor for Nasher's desire to reach out and communicate his enthusiasms. The dominant colour scheme of the identity is green and white, a reference to the verdant lawns that are such an important feature of the museum.

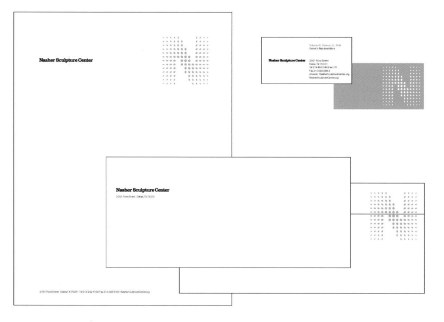

Previous spread, left The Renzo Piano designed Nasher Sculpture Center: illuminating the cultural landscape of downtown Dallas. Founder Ray Nasher chose Piano on the strength of his beautiful building for the Beyeler Foundation, Basel. **Opposite page, top left** Surrounded by skyscrapers, the green lawns and trees of the Nasher provide visitors with a cultural oasis; combined with Piano's architecture, it is the ideal venue for contemporary sculpture and masterpieces of the twentieth century. **Opposite page, top right** The Nasher symbol is informed by Piano's architecture, comprising a 13x13 grid of lozenges, each of which appears to be advancing towards the viewer. The core colour of the identity is green, a reference to the verdant lawns that are such an important feature of the Center. **Opposite page, centre and bottom**

Further print applications of the Nasher identity – designed by New York-based 2x4 – reveal the range of green hues employed. The leaflets and events calendar (centre) are notable for their clarity, the colour palette and typographic language proving incredibly versatile and cohesive. This same clarity can be found on the Nasher's stationery (bottom left), which exudes integrity and restraint. **This page** Assorted print applications, displaying the various cohesive elements of the identity. The core colour palette of green and white is combined with a simple typographic language (a serif font for the Members' Newsletter, a sans serif font for information leaflets and other applications), a decorative palette that employs the dots/lozenges of the logotype and a simple yet evocative photographic language.

The New Art Gallery Walsall
Walsall / UK

The New Art Gallery Walsall

Opened in February 2000, the New Art Gallery Walsall is somewhat unusual among Britain's most recent art spaces in being an entirely new-build project, rather than a refurbished industrial structure. The gallery sits at the head of a redundant canal, its approach lined by chainstores. But for all its mundane melancholy, architects Adam Caruso and Peter St John were excited by the 'democracy and difference' of this urban setting. They responded with a strikingly restrained building that refers to the character of the warehouses and factories that flank the waterway. The gallery houses the Garman Ryan Collection, a body of painting and sculpture donated to the town of Walsall by Jacob Epstein's wife, Kathleen Garman, and a permanent collection of nineteenth-, twentieth- and twenty-first-century art. Alongside maintaining, and adding to, these holdings, it also runs a full programme of temporary exhibitions.

At thirty-seven metres high, Caruso St John's building is visible throughout Walsall and offers residents and visitors a chance to view the town from a new perspective. Working on the identity for the gallery, the graphic designer Jane Chipchase and the design team Michael Nash Associates created a symbol based on its distinctive architectural profile: a rectangular tower broken by a single step. They also designed the custom-font 'Frisky', a digitized version of an old cut of Standard Regular, and named after a sculpture of a dog that is a favourite feature of the permanent collection. The typeface is littered with odd weights and kerning, features intended to help avoid off-putting polish and process in the gallery's communication. To the same end, the designers have taken a fluid approach to the colour scheme and paper stock of the gallery's print collateral. They hope that the identity will be ever-evolving.

The exterior of the Walsall Gallery is wrapped in pale terracotta tiles interrupted by a dispersed pattern of flush windows; inside the dominant materials are wood, concrete and stainless steel. This simple palette has been used to create several series of gallery spaces, each with a different character. The Garman collection is shown in a set of wood-lined rooms of domestic scale, while temporary exhibitions are housed in larger concrete-floored, white-walled galleries. The gallery's interior signage consists of lettering hand-painted on Douglas fir panels and symbols embossed or cut out of leather and wrapped around steel. Rather than merely being attached to the gallery walls, these signs appear to have grown out of the fabric of the building.

Jananne Al-Ani   Nick Crowe
Echolalia Darryl Joe Georgiou
Felix Gonzalez-Torres
Susan Hiller   Kenny Hunter
Alastair Maclennan Gavin Turk
Andrew Tift

22 November 2000 - 21 January 2000
Tuesday - Saturday 10 am - 5 pm Sunday 12 noon - 5 pm
Free Admission Closed Mondays Open Bank Holidays
The New Art Gallery Walsall Gallery Square Walsall
WS2 8LG T 01922 654400 F 01922 654401
www.artatwalsall.org.uk

in memoriam
22.11.2
000-
21.01.2
001

THE ARTS COUNCIL OF ENGLAND   The Henry Moore Foundation   Walsall Metropolitan Borough Council

Previous spread, left The New Art Gallery Walsall, designed by the architects Caruso St John, has not only brought life to the cultural landscape of the area, but is also a striking addition to the town's skyline. **Opposite page** The architectural profile and box-like structure of the gallery lends itself well to interpretation and invention. For this poster promoting the 2001 exhibition 'In Memoriam', the form becomes a coffin, a deadpan reference enriched by the heavy black type. **This page, top and bottom left** The design team took every opportunity to promote and develop the gallery's identity, with the building/logo referenced across a wide range of promotional material including the campaign for the inaugural exhibition, 'Blue' (2000). **This page, top and bottom right** The promotional poster for the exhibition 'Girl' (2000) uses a block of type, top left, to transform the poster into a silhouette of the gallery. The gingham motif and stitched elements communicate the exhibition's theme with just the right amount of wit.

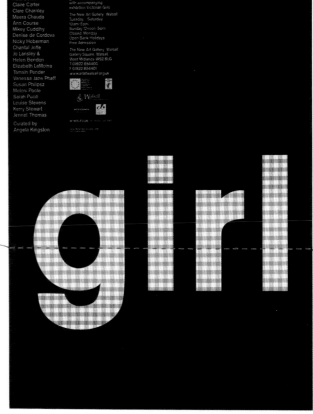

This page, top right The cohesive qualities of the identity system are apparent in these information leaflets. Uniform formats and typography are utilized for the different elements of the communications programme, distinguished by imagery relevant to specific services or periods of programming. This page, top left The design team's presentation included a book of collages detailing their visual inspiration. This example includes one of Damien Hirst's spin paintings and *Frisky*, a statue of a dog that is a favourite feature of the permanent collection. This page, bottom right Stationery is simple and clear, with the logo used as a branding element, most notably for business cards (far right), and as a smaller die-cut element on the edge of letterheads (left) and compliments slips. Opposite page Typography used for the gallery's signage system is consistent with the core identity, while the varied materials are more in harmony with the palette employed for the gallery's interior. Some signs (such as this elevator sign, top left and right) consist of a piece of leather (a local product) wrapped around steel, with cut or embossed lettering. Elsewhere, information has been hand-painted onto Douglas fir panels, while vinyl lettering on windows lists the names of important sponsors (bottom).

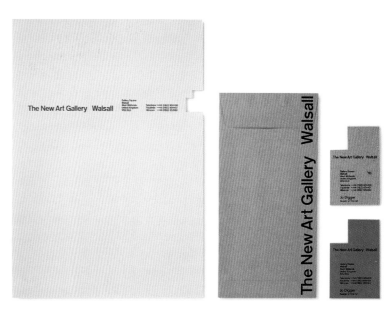

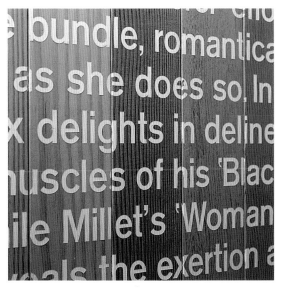

The Garman Ryan Collection has always been arranged thematically, with subjects chosen by Kathleen Garman. This room, therefore, presents pictures with highly contrasting subject matter. However, even within the categories of 'work' and 'leisure', differences appear in the artists' approach. The images of work include both realistic portrayals, and romanticised versions which lack signs of any genuine labour. Joshua Cristall's 'The Bracken Gatherer' effortlessly lifts her huge bundle, romantically framing her face as she does so. In contrast, Delacroix delights in delineating the strong muscles of his 'Blacksmith' at work while Millet's 'Woman Carding Wool' reveals the exertion and drudgery of the woman's task.

Even 'Leisure' is not shown as unalloyed pleasure. While Renoir's 'Country Dance' depicts an enjoyable occasion, Epstein's 'Men with Mice and Birds' has a certain air of menace about it. In 'The Sweat-Shop' he captures a moment of relaxation from dreary toil, skilfully combining the themes of both work and leisure.

The Photographers' Gallery
London/UK

The Photographers'
Gallery

Founded in 1971, the Photographers' Gallery was the first public institution in Britain to be solely devoted to the medium. It was originally located in a converted Lyons teashop at 8 Great Newport Street in central London, a building that now houses the gallery's primary exhibition space and a bookshop. In 1980 the gallery extended into 5 Great Newport Street and these premises currently accommodate a café, a secondary exhibition space and a print sales gallery. The Photographers' Gallery is a not-for-profit organization: it is free to enter and all profits from the bookshop and print sales are ploughed back into the institution.

The gallery was the first venue in London to show major figures such as Jacques Henri Lartigue, Irving Penn and André Kertesz, and more recently it has introduced British audiences to significant contemporary photographers such as Rineke Dijkstra, Annelies Strba, Catherine Opie and Boris Mikhailov. It has also been instrumental in establishing and promoting the names of British photographers, including Martin Parr and Fay Goodwin. Since 1996 the gallery has hosted an annual international photography prize, an award that has become the most prestigious in its field.

For several years the Photographers' Gallery has been planning to expand and refurbish, or to move. The current gallery identity was created by London-based design team North as a 'caretaker identity', an interim solution intended to serve until changes at the gallery prompt a more fundamental rethink. The aim of the design was to introduce consistency across all the gallery's activities at a time when the existing marketing and communications material was very ad hoc. North describe their simple solution as 'non design', an identity without a strong personality that would eventually make way for the development of something more distinctive. It was implemented across the gallery's literature, advertising, marketing, signage, packaging, membership collateral and publishing.

More recent Photographers' Gallery publications have been designed by another London-based team, Spin. Excited by the opportunity to work with spectacular photographic images, Spin have maintained North's method of framing pictures in a clean, restrained manner, allowing the work to come to the fore. They are developing North's strikingly understated design with the introduction of new typographic styles and a broader colour palette. The identity is still in a state of evolution.

Previous spread, left Interior of The Photographers' Gallery. This page, top row Spin has been designing *Great* magazine (the monthly publication covering events and exhibitions at The Photographers' Gallery) since May 2003, creating an ever-evolving though nonetheless cohesive visual language with a bolder typographic palette and dynamic colours aimed at achieving a new sense of purpose. This page, below Catalogue designed by North for 'Asia City' (1998), a collaborative exhibition resulting from the partnership between Asia House and The Photographers' Gallery. Opposite page, top One generic catalogue and slipcase was designed for the Citibank Photography Prize 2001 (left) and 2002 (right). As with the 1998 and 2000 catalogues, North opted for a democratic solution, decorating the slipcases with one of five spine stickers to represent each of the shortlisted photographers. Opposite page, centre A4 format exhibition catalogues for the Citibank Photography Prize. In 1998 North designed a generic catalogue presented in one of five different slipcases, each representing the work of one of the shortlisted photographers, which in 1998 included Thomas Demand (near left) and Andreas Gursky (second from left). The surnames of all the shortlisted photographers were blind embossed on the slipcase. For the 2000 catalogue, the designers removed the slipcase from the equation, designing five different front covers, with a generic back cover sporting the identity conceived for the 2000 prize. Covers shown are for Anna Gaskell (far right) and Jitka Hanzlova (near right).

This page, below left This selection of leaflets and invitations – including invitations to 'Blurred Boundaries', the Citibank Photography Prize and exhibitions by Erwin Wurm, Corinne Day, Malerie Marder and John Hoppy Hopkins – reveals the importance of colour to the identity system developed for The Photographers' Gallery by North. **This page, below right** The clarity of the identity system is again apparent in these leaflets designed to promote the gallery's print sales service and the Print Circle (now the Patrons' Group).

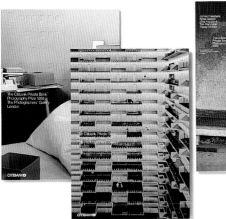

The Public Theater
New York / USA

The Public Theater was founded by the producer Joseph Papp in 1967. Based in the refurbished nineteenth-century Astor Library on Lafayette Street, between Soho and the East Village, it evolved from Papp's New York Shakespeare Festival, an annual season of free open-air performances as a gift to the city. The first performance at the theatre was the world premiere of the musical *Hair*. Markedly un-Shakespearian, it established Papp's vision of presenting drama of all sorts to audiences that went beyond the traditional Broadway crowds.

Papp drove The Public Theater for two decades, garnering awards and an international reputation. His identification with the institution was such that, on his death in 1991, it suffered a significantly uncertain period. The momentum of Papp's golden years – years when the theatre played host to writers such as Sam Shepherd and David Mamet – was only regained in the mid-1990s under the new leadership of playwright/director George C. Wolfe. Adopting the abbreviated name 'The Public', Wolfe emphatically took up Papp's pursuit of a non-traditional theatre audience.

Although Papp had commissioned a series of distinctive posters from illustrator Paul Davis, he had never given The Public Theater a formal visual identity. Starting from scratch, Wolfe chose, instead of plunging headfirst into a full graphic overhaul, to hire Paula Scher of Pentagram for the immediate task of designing the promotion for the 1994 Shakespeare Festival. Inspired by Victorian playbills, Scher's solution was to generate drama through typographic means. She used fonts based on various weights of wood type to present pure information in an eye-catching fashion.

Scher's advertisements were an immediate success and, given the direct nature of their appeal, their relationship with the notion of 'the Public' was apparent. Commissioned by the newly confident Wolfe to extend these designs to the theatre as a whole, she created the now well-known variegated wood-type logo and a series of roundels representing the other activities and venues that come under the auspices of the institution. Since then, Scher has worked with an in-house designer generating numerous posters, advertisements, programmes and signage for the theatre.

To an extent, Scher's identity for The Public has been a victim of its own success. Becoming a default graphic style for would-be edgy theatre, the designer was disconcerted to find lookalike typography on posters for Broadway productions such as the musical *Chicago*. In order to convey the innovative nature of The Public Theater's productions, Scher has begun to combine the singular identity with an ever-changing spectrum of graphic styles, and currently each performance at The Public is promoted with custom-designed typography. The only consistent elements remain the logo and the combined visions of Scher and Wolfe, who between them nurture a sturdy appreciation of populism.

Previous spread, left The visual language created for The Public Theater by Paula Scher and her team suited the streets of Manhattan. One campaign that caught the public's imagination was *Bring in da Noise, Bring in da Funk*, for which the designers choreographed a vibrant visual vocabulary with heavy sans serif type, animated imagery and a palette of bright colours. **This page, top** In recent years, the graphic language employed to promote the theatre's various events has been refined and updated, incorporating an ever-widening palette of tools, suggesting that the theatre itself is evolving. The poster for *Much Ado About Nothing*, part of the Shakespeare in Central Park season, invoked a more magical atmosphere than previous Public Theater posters, suggesting the time of year (summer), location and the play itself. **This page, bottom row** The typographic language employed for The Public Theater's promotional campaigns has varied over the years and includes the block serif font used to great effect for *The Story* and *Guinea Pig Solo*, and the uppercase sans serif used for *As You Like It*. **Opposite page** Promotional poster for the New York Shakespeare Festival's 2003 production of *Henry V*. This poster is a fine example of how the visual language has evolved over the years, with simple, modernist sans serif type and a bold, minimal colour scheme replacing the evocative letterpress type employed in earlier campaigns.

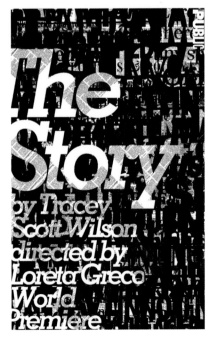

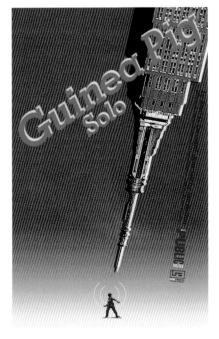

Shakespeare's Globe Theatre
London / UK

Shakespeare's Globe Theatre is a reproduction of the theatre where Shakespeare worked in the early seventeenth century, and for which he wrote many of his best-known plays. Designed by architect Theo Crosby and opened nearly four centuries after the original, the theatre is as faithful as possible in every aspect, but for its compliance with contemporary health and safety regulations. The Globe began life as the project of actor Sam Wanamaker, who established the Shakespeare Globe Trust in 1970. The foundations of the theatre were laid in 1987 on London's South Bank, on a site that is a mere 200 yards from that of the original Globe. Sadly Wanamaker died only months after construction of the auditorium began in 1993, but his work continued and the theatre opened for its first season in the summer of 1997.

Under the founding artistic directorship of Mark Rylance, the emphasis of a large part of the Globe's performances and educational activity has been to explore the tension between experiment and reconstruction. As well as offering groundbreaking interpretations of plays by Shakespeare and his contemporaries, the theatre has staged a number of new works, particularly those written by authors writing with the conditions of the theatre in mind. Rather than being a touristic curiosity, the Globe has become one of London's most exciting performance spaces.

The Globe commissions new designers for each season and project, and is therefore able to present a varied graphic front that is in keeping with the dynamism of its dramatic agenda. Working on the marketing material for the 2003 season, the design team GTF chose to confront the paradoxes of pursuing original Elizabethan theatrical practice in the twenty-first century. In particular, they explored the manner in which the Globe's emphasis on original practice extends beyond what is seen by the audience into elements such as stage management and costume design. The key component of the design is a series of photographs by Nigel Shafran. Half-posed and taken in natural light, these images map the confrontation and interchange between the extraordinary environment of the theatre and the outside world.

That same year the theatre published the book *Play*, a document and celebration of its first five seasons. Designed by Pentagram partner Angus Hyland and designer Charlie Hanson, the book employs a dual typographic system: Minion to reflect the Globe's Elizabethan origins and Helvetica Neue to communicate its contemporary agenda. The book was printed on coarse natural stock, which, as well as rendering it a satisfying object, also imbues it with a non-specific sense of history. Hyland commissioned a series of pattern-based illustrations to introduce each of the theatre's annual seasons. These include intricately woven Celtic imagery prefacing 'The Celtic Season' of 2001, and a series of columns and architectural details announcing 1999's 'The Roman Season'.

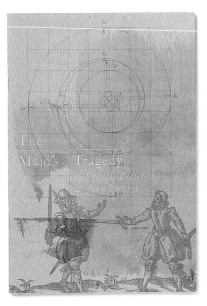

The
Maid's Tragedy
by Francis Beaumont
& John Fletcher

The
Winter's Tale
by William Shakespeare

The life
of Henry the Fift
by William Shakespeare

As you Like it
by William Shakespeare

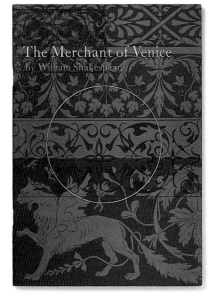

The Merchant of Venice
by William Shakespeare

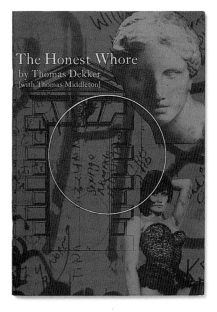

The Honest Whore
by Thomas Dekker
[with Thomas Middleton]

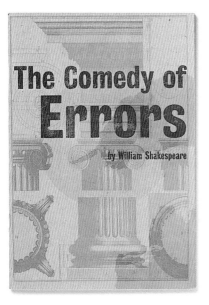

The Comedy of
Errors
by William Shakespeare

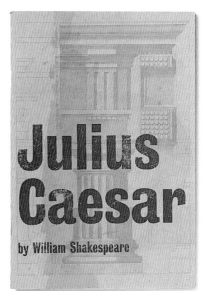

Julius
Caesar
by William Shakespeare

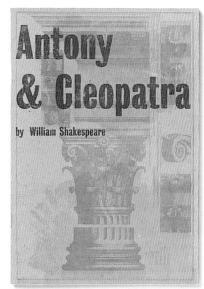

Antony
& Cleopatra
by William Shakespeare

Previous spread, left Backstage at the Globe. Actors in Elizabethan costume relax with a cup of tea and catch up with the news in this Nigel Shafran photograph, employed for the 2003 promotional campaign. **Opposite page** Programmes for the first three seasons at the rebuilt Globe, all designed by Angus Hyland of Pentagram. For 1997's 'Opening Season' (top), the programmes employ layered engravings and illustrations to form a tapestry of suitably evocative imagery. Type was embossed and foil-blocked in gold, as it was for 1998's 'Season of Justice and Mercy' (centre), the darker colour palette referring to the season's subject matter. For 1999's 'Roman Season' (bottom), Hyland both lightened and broadened his palette, with layered architectural drawings of columns and heavy letterpress type suggesting the pomp and vigour of the Roman Empire. **This page, top** Programme covers from 2004's 'The Season of Star-Crossed Lovers'. The evocative photography of Nigel Shafran moves beyond the inner-sanctum of the performers and the performance arena, documenting crowds of people outside the theatre walls, acknowledging the role of the audience. **This page, bottom** Programme covers from 2003's 'The Season of Regime Change'. The designers chose to present Shafran's photographs of the theatre, albeit ones absent of people, a visual metaphor suggesting an empty throne.

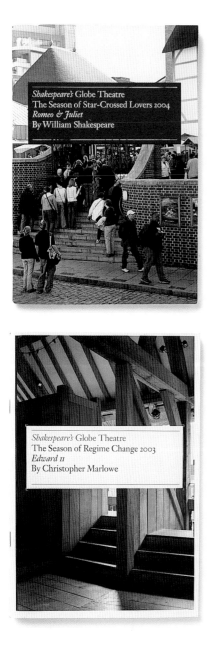

Opposite page *Play* – published to document and celebrate the first five seasons at the rebuilt Shakespeare's Globe Theatre – was designed to express the sense of history one associates with the Globe, as well as its place in London's contemporary cultural landscape. A strong photographic language, including full-bleed performance images, is complemented by the illustrations used to introduce each chapter/season. **This page** For posters promoting 2004's 'The Season of Star-Crossed Lovers' (top left) and 2003's 'The Season of Regime Change' (top right), the designers emphasized the role of the performers, awaiting or preparing for performance. For these A5 flyers – for *Edward II* (bottom right) and *Twelfth Night* (bottom left) – the team at GTF chose close-cropped images of performers on-stage to suggest a sense of drama.

Shakespeare's Globe Theatre

The Season of Star-Crossed Lovers
Much Ado About Nothing
Measure for Measure
Romeo & Juliet
700 × £5 tickets at
every show

7 May–26 September 2004
Tickets 020 7401 9919 / 020 7850 8590
Bankside, London SE1
www.shakespeares-globe.org

Shakespeare's Globe Theatre
Richard II, Richard III, Edward II,
The Taming of the Shrew
& Dido, Queen of Carthage
600 × £5 tickets
at every performance

8 May–28 September 2003
Tickets 020 7401 9919 / 020 7850 8590
Bankside, London SE1
www.shakespeares-globe.org

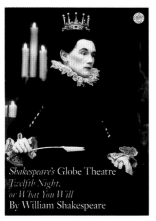

Shakespeare's Globe Theatre
Twelfth Night,
or What You Will
By William Shakespeare

Shakespeare's Globe Theatre
Twelfth Night,
or What You Will
By William Shakespeare

Shakespeare's Globe Theatre
Edward II
By Christopher Marlowe

Shakespeare's Globe Theatre
The Season of Regime Change
Edward II
By Christopher Marlowe

Stedelijk Museum CS
Amsterdam / Netherlands

The Stedelijk Museum's established premises on Amsterdam's Museum Square were closed in January 2004 to allow for refurbishment and extension. This programme was expected to take at least four years and in the interim the museum opened in a temporary location on the second and third floors of the Post-CS building, near Amsterdam's Central Station and formerly used for sorting mail. Experimental Jetset were commissioned to create the graphic design specifically for the new location. In keeping with the temporary nature of the site, which was originally leased to the museum for only three years, they generated an identity and signage system that is direct, inexpensive and flexible. The abbreviation of the museum's full title to the initials SMCS emphasizes the need for immediacy that permeates the entire project.

The form of the SMCS logotype was originally inspired by the pattern on airmail envelopes, an allusion to the building's former use. As the project developed, this reference to the postal system gave way to a host of other concerns, but the red and blue colour scheme and the diagonal stripes were retained for a variety of reasons. While the colour red relates the identity to that of the original Stedelijk Museum, the blue offers an extreme contrast, suggesting that SMCS is a bold new curatorial venture as well as a temporary home. Using the colours side by side in diagonal stripes, Experimental Jetset created a pattern that they believe is analogous to the dialectic that is at work in the museum itself. In a related vein, the designers have deployed the diagonal stripes that form the logotype in a manner that allows the individual characters to fluctuate between representation and abstraction. The result is a permanently unfixed logo, a design that acts as another metaphor for the state of the museum.

The basis of the signage system used inside SMCS is the cheapest and most generic of graphic display materials: the A4 plastic document holder. Gathered into grids of various dimensions, these see-through envelopes are transformed into the units of a low-cost, flexible, easy-to-use scheme. Although the impulse behind the system was practical, Experimental Jetset chose to blow it up to near absurd proportions by using 2,000 envelopes in the building overall. As such, it becomes a gesture of exaggerated ordinariness of the kind associated with Pop Art. The typeface employed in the system is Univers, designed in 1952 by Adrian Frutiger. Used throughout the museum during the directorship of graphic designer Wim Crouwel, this face is strongly associated with the Stedelijk.

As well as creating the identity for SMCS, Experimental Jetset have also redesigned the institution's quarterly *Stedelijk Museum Bulletin*, a magazine that is sent to patrons and sold in bookshops. Once again they use the red and blue colour scheme, but in this instance the design relates to the museum as a whole, not just its temporary location. Significantly, the pages of the Bulletin have none of the sketchy intermediate qualities that characterize the graphic presentation of SMCS.

Previous spread, left Interior signage for 20/20 Vision, a group show concerned with visual culture. The 20/20 Vision logotype was applied in different sizes, a reference to optical tests, whilst the diagonal of the slash echoes the core SMCS logo. **Opposite page** Interior signage comprises A4 sheets of paper held in plastic folders, underlining the temporary character of the location. It is a practical system that is both time and cost efficient, as information can be replaced and/or updated whenever necessary. The designers revelled in the disposable qualities of the system, using 2000 sleeves throughout the building. **This page** Posters designed to promote the launch of the Stedelijk's temporary home, announcing the opening date of the venue (16 May) with a huge figure 16 set in the diagonal stripes of the SMCS mark, a visual theme repeated in the layout of the 'Open daily!' poster (left).

This page, top left Issue 03 of the *Stedelijk Bulletin*. Published quarterly, it is a manifestation of the Stedelijk Museum rather than the SMCS, so it was essential that the designers retain the integrity of the core identity, while simultaneously promoting the temporary space. The redesigned magazine refers to its own history: two black dots at the spine recall the original *Bulletin* of the 1960s, issues of which could be collected in a special ring binder. **This page, top, centre** Cover and opening page from Issue 04 of the *Bulletin*. The opening page (left) shows a poster designed

by Jop van Bennekom (2004) for an annual exhibition of the Municipal Art Acquisitions; the spotlight in 2004 was on graphic design acquisitions. The front cover (right) uses one of the new acquisitions to great effect, namely *Untitled (Never Judge a Book by Its Cover)* by goodwill (Will Holder). **This page, top, far right** The simplicity and basic, temporary feel of the identity is carried across all relevant manifestations of the SMCS identity, including these small notebooks which are sold in the SMCS shop. **This page, bottom** The full logotype and four

variations of the SMCS mark (left) and an exhibitions and events leaflet for May–December 2004 (right). The colour palette employed by the designers lends itself well to the layered presentation of information: Dutch exhibition and event titles are set in red with English translations in blue, while dates are set in black. **Opposite page** Signage graphics at the entrance to SMCS (top) are bold, bright, and remain clear, even at a distance. A more expansive shot of the SMCS entrance (bottom) exhibits the restrained, industrial nature of the Stedelijk's temporary home.

Théâtre d'Angoulême
Scène Nationale
Angoulême / France

Housed in a nineteenth-century building, Le Théâtre d'Angoulême is an important and well-loved civic feature of the south-western French town of Angoulême. The interior was extensively refurbished in the late 1990s, but the exterior was preserved and restored in keeping with local sentiment. In 1991 the theatre was designated a Scène Nationale and, hence, brought into a network of institutions dedicated to supporting live performances of all kinds. The structure of the theatre may be traditional, but the performances – whether drama, dance or music – are generally innovative. The mission of Angoulême is to support contemporary activity and nurture the repertoire of the future.

The graphic designers Annette Lenz and Vincent Perrottet began working for the theatre on the arrival of its current director Joël Gunzburger in 2001. Lenz and Perrottet had both designed materials for Gunzburger when he worked at a theatre in Rungis, near Paris. At that time the designers were working independently, and the idea of their collaboration was initiated by Gunzburger, who was keen on the work of both designers and unwilling to choose between them.

Lenz and Perrottet's first decision was not to change the logotype of the theatre. Designed several years previously by the studio of Thérèses Troïka, they recognized that it was well-crafted, easy to use and was already widely recognized both locally and among the broader theatre community. Incorporating Troïka's logo, they currently design new graphic material for each season, including information leaflets, posters and invitations. Given the theatre's very varied programme, their main task is to create a strong core identity without obscuring the sense of diversity. Gunzburger and his head of communication, Marie-Christine Léger, both recognize that the poster is an independent cultural form and, as such, they allow Lenz and Perrottet a significant amount of creative freedom. So long as they work within the modest resources of the theatre, the designers are encouraged to create strong images that not only sell performances, but also provoke and engage. The identity of Le Théâtre d'Angoulême is a work in progress, with Lenz and Perrottet generating a new set of graphic motifs each year.

Previous spread, left The glass doors at the theatre's entrance proved to be the perfect medium for exploring the possibilities of the predominantly typographic design language, with the names of past productions set in varying sizes to communicate the theatre's dynamic approach to programming. **Opposite page** Annette Lenz and Vincent Perrottet designed these posters, to promote the 2004–2005 season, with clarity and élan, despite the rather complex visual language employed by the designers to suggest the theatre's reputation for staging innovative productions. It also complements and reflects the visual language of the existing logotype (designed by the Thérèses Troïka studio). **This page** Two posters from a series promoting the 2003–2004 season. Like the posters designed for the following season (opposite), these employ a fractured, three-dimensional language, with a folded band bearing dates and information moving from the top of the poster to the bottom. The band sits on top of a flat photographic image evoking the time of year, elements of which are integrated into the information band itself.

Vitra Design Museum
Weil am Rhein / Germany

Vitra Design Museum

The Vitra Design Museum (VDM) in Weil am Rhein was originally established as a venue for exhibiting the company's collection and new products to clients, friends and the media. The idea of turning what is essentially a private design collection into a public institution had few precedents and the museum is largely the vision of Vitra Chairman Dr Rolf Fehlbaum. Working closely with founding director Alexander von Vegesack, Fehlbaum opened the doors of his Frank Gehry-designed museum (Gehry's first building in Europe) in November 1989.

VDM concentrates on design and architecture exhibitions that are not only developed for its space, but also designed to travel to venues world-wide. Its exhibitions have been mounted in prestigious institutions including the Museum of Modern Art in New York, the Centre Georges Pompidou in Paris and London's Design Museum. As well as communicating the museum's message abroad, travelling exhibits generate the funds with which the VDM maintains its busy programme. This includes two or three new exhibitions each year, an active acquisitions policy (the VDM has increased its holdings by nearly 200% over the last fifteen years), workshops run in partnership with the Pompidou, the maintenance of an extensive archive and a publishing programme that keeps pace with the exhibitions.

Wanting the museum to benefit from its connection to Vitra, Fehlbaum developed an identity that was related to that of the company. The Vitra logotype (the same for company and museum) was in place from the begin-ning, but the design of the print and the promotional material evolved over the VDM's first year. Initially the graphic design was developed on an exhibi-tion-by-exhibition basis, but later, under the management of designer Torsten Romanus, a strong, coherent language was established. Romanus continues to design most of the VDM's graphics, from print to signage and wall graphics. Allowing each exhibition to bear the stamp of its subject, his aim is to be consistent in tone without being rigid in style.

Alongside VDM's Gehry building, its colourful yet sensible graphic style and its travelling exhibits, another important element of the museum's identity is its merchandising. In particular the miniature models of Vitra's best-known chairs have proved hugely popular. As well as emblems for those who can't afford or don't have room to house the real thing, they are accurate enough to be used as examples in product design classes.

The most important task of the VDM's identity is to reconcile the promo-tion of the museum as an independent cultural force with the exploitation of its relationship to the company. Those at the museum admit that this is a balancing act, but point to the consistently high standard of the VDM's exhibitions as emphatic evidence of their success.

TRANSPORTING

In addition to interior objects that have handles or wheels for the purpose of mobility, this group includes objects that are self-propelled or coupled with other means of transportation. Thomas Warren's resilient swivel chair on wheels, which is based on a patent for seating in American railroad cars, and the folding armchair designed by Raymond Loewy for a train compartment, represent an entire spectrum of interiors in transportation vehicles with domestic characteristics. Indeed, virtually every type of vehicle – from the horse-drawn carriage to the jetliner – has also been used as a dwelling. Even cooking facilities, heating and lighting, which we typically think of as permanent installations, have existed in mobile versions for centuries.

Deployed shell = Vanishing of passerbys' speeds. Diving into intimate time

DESIGN SOLLTE MÖGLICHST VIELEN SO VIEL VOM BESTEN WIE MÖGLICH

Previous spread, left The Vitra Design Museum at Weil am Rhein was designed by Frank O. Gehry, his first work in Europe, and opened to the public in November 1989. **Opposite page** Each Vitra Design Museum exhibition is conceived as a travelling show. Designed by Dieter Thiel – who also designs Vitra's furniture showrooms and has designed Vitra furniture with Mario Bellini – each exhibition has to be flexible in structure and layout, as well as being strong enough on content, to be accommodated in anything up to four or five different venues worldwide. **This page, top** The visual language employed by the graphic designer for the museum's promotional programmes and publications reflects and supports the modernist simplicity of the identity. Typography is clear whilst colour palettes are striking yet unfussy, such as the programme developed for the Marcel Breuer retrospective 'Design und Architektur' (2003–2004). **This page, bottom left** Catalogue for 'Airworld' (2004–2005), a touring exhibition dedicated to the 'airworld' encountered by airline passengers from the perspective of the history of design and architecture. **This page, bottom right** A much more restrained and pared down language was employed for the catalogue published to accompany the 2003–2004 exhibition 'Die Wohnkulturen der arabischen Welt' (Domestic Cultures in the Arab World).

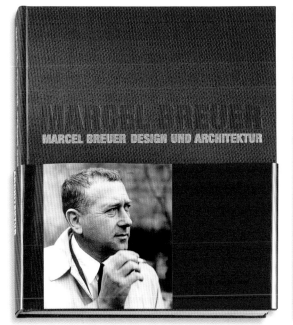

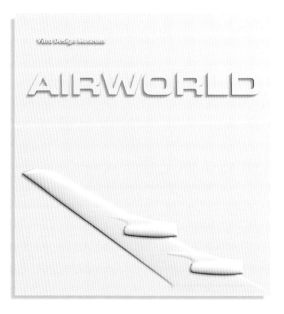

Walker Art Center
Minneapolis/USA

WALKER ART CENTER

Established in 1927, the Walker Art Center in Minneapolis has always been a pioneering institution. It was the first public art gallery in the region and, in the 1940s, it became one of the earliest museums to focus on modern art, collecting works by, amongst others, Picasso, Moore and Giacometti. Since then it has evolved into a thoroughly integrated multidisciplinary arts venue, one which serves as a model for organizations worldwide. The Walker simultaneously maintains a permanent collection and runs a full programme of temporary exhibitions, dance, theatre and music performances, film screenings and educational workshops and events.

In February 2004 the Walker closed for a year as part of a programme of expansion and refurbishment. It opened again in 2005 with a new Herzog & de Meuron-designed building and improved facilities including new gallery space and a theatre, as well as visitor amenities such as a restaurant, a shop and below-ground parking. A key feature of the new design is a 'town square', a large open space intended to promote community interaction, both programmed and spontaneous. During its year-long closure, the Walker conducted a series of shows and events under the banner 'Walker Without Walls'. These took place across the area, from the neighbouring Minneapolis Sculpture Garden to far-flung reaches of the Twin Cities region. It was an experiment that proved a resounding success and the Walker aims to integrate the lessons learned from it into its future programming.

Since 1995 the Walker has used the Matthew Carter-designed 'Walker' typeface in place of a more conventionally defined logo. Characterized by snap-on multi-form serifs, this face is uniquely flexible, and the identity of the centre became a function of constant typographic variation. Walker was adapted by the Design Director Andrew Blauvelt for use during the 'Walker Without Walls' period and then later reworked for the 2005 reopening. The premise of the latest design is that a 'font' need not be a set of individual characters, but can be a collection of phrases, each of which correlates to a keyboard command. Working with Walker and other faces, the type designer Eric Olsen developed four 'dialects', i.e. keyboard-responsive sets of terms that refer to different areas of the Walker's activities. Called Public A, Public B, Peer-to-Peer and Intradepartmental, these categories amount to a hierarchical breakdown of the institutional tone of voice.

In its printed, environmental and on-screen applications, the Walker's word fonts are used to create ribbons of terms. These are either presented straightforwardly against solid white or black bands or, more decoratively, against colours and patterns. These varying modes allow the Walker's in-house design team to move from the simple to the complex and from the generic to the custom in their application of the new identity. The source of the patterns was photographic documentation of Walker events, and the exuberance they create relates to the extroversion and animation of Herzog & de Meuron's new structure. The aim was to create a mode of expression equivalent to the Walker's new architectural spirit.

CONCEPT: A NEW "FONT" IN WHICH ONE LETTER = ONE WORD.

F. 4
DESIGN   DEVELOPMENT & MEMBERSHIP   DIRECTOR'S OFFICE   VISUAL ARTS   MINNEAPOLIS SCULPTURE GARDEN   FILM/VIDEO   REGISTRATION   LIBRARY/ARCHIVES   MARKETING & PUBLIC RELATIONS   NEW MEDIA INITIATIVES   PERFORMING ARTS   EDUCATION & COMMUNITY PROGRAMS   WALKER SHOP
F. 3
DESIGN   DEVELOPMENT & MEMBERSHIP   DIRECTOR'S OFFICE   VISUAL ARTS   WALKER ART CENTER   MINNEAPOLIS SCULPTURE GARDEN   FILM/VIDEO   REGISTRATION   WALKER ART CENTER   LIBRARY/ARCHIVES   MARKETING & PUBLIC RELATIONS   NEW MEDIA INITIATIVES   WALKER ART CENTER   PERFORMING ARTS   EDUCATION & COMMUNITY PROGRAMS   WALKER SHOP
F. 2
EXHIBITIONS   DANCE   INTERACTIVE   LECTURES   PAINTING   MUSIC   TOURS   FILM   SCULPTURE   THEATER   DIGITAL ART   CLASSES   ARCHITECTURE   MINNEAPOLIS SCULPTURE GARDEN   WORKSHOPS   SCREENINGS   TALKS   VIDEO   PHOTOGRAPHY   PERFORMANCE
F. 1
EXHIBITIONS   DANCE   INTERACTIVE   LECTURES   WALKER ART CENTER   PAINTING   MUSIC   TOURS   FILM   SCULPTURE   WALKER ART CENTER   THEATER   DIGITAL ART   CLASSES   ARCHITECTURE   WALKER ART CENTER   MINNEAPOLIS SCULPTURE GARDEN   WORKSHOPS   SCREENINGS   WALKER ART CENTER   TALKS   VIDEO   PHOTOGRAPHY   PERFORMANCE

Previous spread, left Established in 1927, the Walker Art Center has occupied its current home – designed by Edward Larrabee Barnes – since 1971. The new Walker identity was prompted by the expansion of the centre. Designed by Herzog & de Meuron and opened in February 2005, the extension (pictured) has doubled the size of the Walker. Opposite page, top An image showing one of the new identity's core visual elements – a 'tape' or 'ribbon' of terms – in use as a signage element in the Walker's car parks. Opposite page, bottom Diagram showing how the new font ('in which one letter = one word') is composed, the premise being that 'a "font" need not be a set of individual characters, but can be a collection of phrases, each of which correlates to a keyboard command.' The diagram is taken from the Walker Design Studio's presentation of the new identity: an identity 'as language'. This page Colour and subtle decorative elements can be introduced to the ribbons of language, when appropriate, to render the identity either 'simple and basic' or 'fanciful and complex'.

THE IDENTITY CAN BE SIMPLE AND BASIC, OR...

...FANCIFUL AND COMPLEX...

This page The new Walker identity in a selection of its more animated manifestations, including bags and merchandise for the Walker's shop. The consistency of the new identity can be found in the typeface itself – Walker, designed by Matthew Carter – and in the broad, albeit uniform, palette of colours. **Opposite page, top** Image taken from the Walker Design Studio's presentation introducing the new identity. **Opposite page, bottom** Stationery applications of the flexible, evolving identity with several options provided for consideration, from clean and simple to complex, more decorative interpretations.

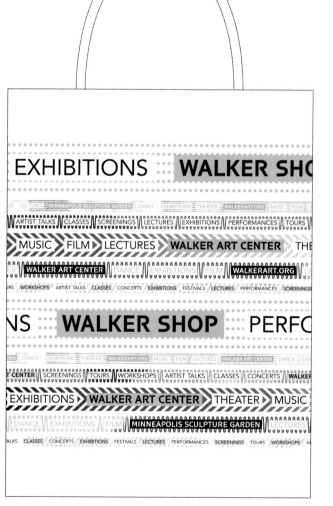

IMAGINE THE IDENTITY LIKE A ROLL OF TAPE—A STRING OF WORDS— THAT CAN BE APPLIED TO ANY SURFACE.

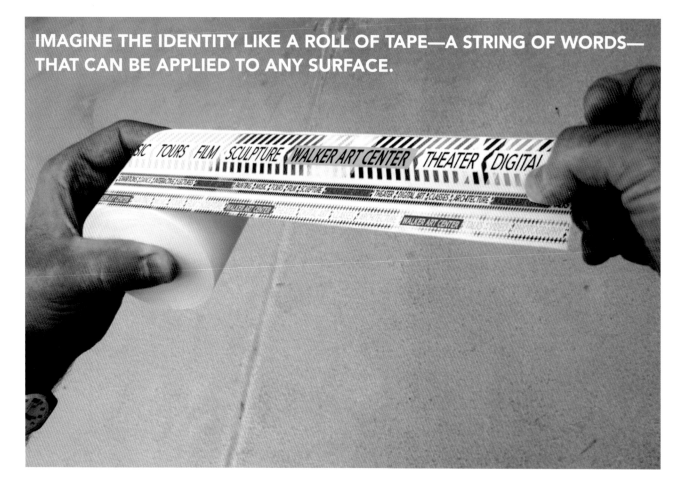

The Whitechapel Art Gallery
London / UK

Whitechapel

The Whitechapel Art Gallery opened in 1901 in a purpose-built Arts and Crafts building on Whitechapel High Street, designed by Charles Harrison Townsend. Its mission was to bring art to the East End, one of London's least prosperous districts. The gallery's first exhibition included works by the Pre-Raphaelites, Constable, Hogarth and Rubens, and drew crowds of local residents. In 1932 the Whitechapel established East End Academy, an open submission show for artists working in the area. Later called the Whitechapel Open, but recently reverting to its original title, this exhibition has become a central fixture in the gallery's programme, enjoying an increasingly high profile due to the number of artists moving into the neighbourhood. Artists featured in the Whitechapel Open include Anthony Gormley, Cornelia Parker, Richard Wentworth, Rachel Whiteread and Alison Wilding.

In the 1980s the Whitechapel went through a programme of refurbishment under the directorship of Nicholas Serota. Closing the galleries for over a year, architects John Miller and Partners stripped out the interiors to create a series of large, bright spaces appropriate for showing contemporary art. In tandem with the building work, graphic designer Peter Saville designed a new identity to announce the gallery's reopening in 1985. Responding to the nature of the new galleries, it featured a typeface with a classical outer line and an unadorned minimal interior. When Iwona Blazwick was appointed Director in 2001, the galleries were much as they had been in the mid-1980s, but the Saville identity had been discontinued for some time. Blazwick commissioned design team Spin to generate a new design with the aim of re-establishing the Whitechapel's position at the centre of contemporary culture. The gallery was looking for something visually distinct that would have as much resonance with local audiences as with the international art world.

Spin's solution for the gallery was to spell out the name 'Whitechapel' in a typeface built from a fine grid of squares. This typeface can be extended to title shows or to create headlines, and its geometrical building blocks can also function in a less direct, more suggestive fashion. Spin's extremely flexible identity allows for a wide number of applications and also for a degree of development and evolution, but thus far the gallery has chosen to use it in a more limited scope, primarily applying it to exhibition signage and print advertisements. The identity is high-tech and busy, yet also non-aggressive. Spin's aim is to reflect both the diversity of the Whitechapel's locale and the dynamism of international contemporary art. Since its launch in 2003, the gridded typeface has announced shows by artists including Cristina Iglesias, Philip-Lorca di Corcia and Gerhard Richter.

Previous spread, left The gallery, an important asset to the neighbourhood, is usually referred to simply as the Whitechapel. The new logotype acknowledges both of these factors. **Opposite page, above** Gallery information graphics, including a calendar of events and information on current and future shows. The glass case recalls the golden age of galleries and museums, whilst also providing a flexible option for the display of information. **Opposite page, below** Events leaflet from late 2003. The focus here is on the image – taken from the exhibition 'Franzwestite: Franz West Works' 1973–2003 – with type set vertically in a thin band of colour on the right-hand side, revealing the versatility and legibility of the logotype. **This page, above** Events leaflet for late 2002/early 2003. Although still an integral element of the visual language, the impact of the image is reduced while the gallery's identity is pushed to the fore. Colour plays an important role in the Whitechapel identity, the broad band of yellow on this leaflet providing an energetic ground for the logotype. **This page, below** Poster for Philip-Lorca di Corcia's 2003 exhibition, 'A Storybook Life'. Although the image is given precedence here – full-bleed with white text – the 'branding' of the venue is clear. The logotype is large, though far from intrusive, whilst the artist's name and the dates of the exhibition are set in the Whitechapel font, maintaining the clarity and coherence of the identity.

Editor/Design Director: Angus Hyland, Pentagram Design
Assistant Editor: Steven Bateman, Pentagram Design
Text and interviews: Emily King
Designer: Zara Moore, Pentagram Design

Acknowledgements

American Folk Art Museum, New York, USA Woody Pirtle and team at Pentagram **BALTIC: The Centre for Contemporary Art, Gateshead, UK** Cathryn Rowley, Nina Byrne and Craig Astley at BALTIC; Henrik Nygren and Greger Ulf Nilson; Lillemor Ronnback; Jonas Bergqvist; Etienne Clèment; Ripe, Gateshead **BAM: Brooklyn Academy of Music, New York, USA** Michael Bierut and team at Pentagram **Cass Sculpture Foundation, Goodwood & London, UK** Ben Parker at Made Thought; Daniel Weil and team at Pentagram; Mark Cass, Wilfred Cass, and the Cass Sculpture Foundation; Nick Turner **CDDB Théâtre de Lorient, Lorient, France** Michael Amzalag & Mathias Augustyniak at M/M Paris **Centre National de la Danse, Pantin, France** Karine Atencia and Agathe Poupeny at CND; Pierre Vormeringer and Annette Lucas at Atalante Paris; Pierre di Sciulio **Fondazione Querini Stampalia, Venice, Italy** Karin and Sebastiano Girardi at Studio Camuffo (Venice) **Frieze Art Fair, London, UK** Graphic Thought Facility **Gagosian Gallery, New York/Los Angeles/London, USA/UK** Peter Blythe, Judith McKay and Kelsey Finlayson at Bruce Mau Design; Brad Kaye at Gagosian Gallery; Vanessa Beecroft; Richard Hamilton; Ed Ruscha; Richard Serra; Mark di Suvero **La Ferme du Buisson, Marne-La-Vallée, France** Florence Jacob et Maroussia Janelle; Melanie Drouere and Louis Janaud at La Ferme du Buisson **Lakeland Arts Trust, Cumbria, UK** Edward King and Sandy Kitching at Lakeland Arts Trust; Angus Hyland and team, Pentagram **Mobile Home Gallery, London, UK** Ronnie Simpson, Director, Mobile Home Gallery; Julie Verhoeven; Roxy Walsh; Jonathan Barnbrook at Barnbrook Design **Moderna Museet, Stockholm, Sweden** Catrin Lindstrom and Titti Kurppa at Stockholm Design Lab; Henrik Nygren and Greger Ulf Nilson **MoMA QNS, New York, USA** Natasha Jen, Cecilie von Haffner and Steven Mosier at Base Design New York **Mori Art Museum, Tokyo, Japan** Jonathan Barnbrook and Pedro Inoue, Barnbrook Design; David Elliott and Mina Takahashi, Mori Art Museum **Museo Nacional del Prado, Madrid, Spain** Miguel Zugaza, Director, Prado; Fernando Gutiérrez, Pentagram; Miquel Garay (art director) and German Simone (designer) at the Prado; Photographers Ana Nance and Rick Dávila **Museum Boijmans van Beuningen, Rotterdam, Netherlands** Armand Mevis **Museum of Contemporary Art San Diego, La Jolla/San Diego, USA** Laurie Chambliss, Anne Farrell, Lehze Flax at MCASD; Michael Rock and Susan Sellers at 2x4 **Museum für Gegenwartskunst Siegen, Siegen, Germany** Uwe Loesch **MuseumsQuartier Wien, Vienna, Austria** Daniela Enzi at MQ; Andreas Miedaner and Gertraud Haas at Büro X Design GmbH **Nasher Sculpture Center, Dallas, USA** Michael Rock and Susan Sellers at 2x4; Michel Denance **The New Art Gallery Walsall, Walsall, UK** Richard Hales at Michael Nash Associates; Jane Chipchase; Emily Pitt at Caruso St John Architects; Helene Binet **The Photographers' Gallery, London, UK** Sean Perkins, Fi McGhee and Stephen Gilmore, North; Ben Fergusson at The Photographers' Gallery **The Public Theater, New York, USA** Paula Scher and team at Pentagram **Shakespeare's Globe Theatre, London, UK** Tiffany Foster at the Shakespeare's Globe Theatre; Graphic Thought Facility; Nigel Shafran; Angus Hyland and team, Pentagram **Stedelijk Museum CS, Amsterdam, Netherlands** Erwin Brinkers, Marieke Stolk and Danny van Dungen, Experimental Jetset **Théâtre d'Angoulême Scène Nationale, Angoulême, France** Annette Lenz and Vincent Perrottet **Vitra Design Museum, Weil am Rhein, Germany** Mathias Schwartz-Clauss and Alexa Tepen at Vitra Design Museum **Walker Art Center, Minneapolis, USA** Andrew Blauvelt and Chad Kloepfer at Walker Art Center **The Whitechapel Art Gallery, London, UK** Tony Brook, Patricia Finegan and Joseph at Spin; Rachel Mappleback at The Whitechapel

We would also like to thank Fi McGee; Rory McGrath; Maureen Mooren and Daniel van der Velde; Jan Mot; Paul Boudens; Elisa Uematsu; First Edition Translations; Supernatural Studios; Sharon Hwang; Fabian Herrmann; Kurt Koepfle and Brian Smith at Pentagram; Daisy Mallabar, Press Office, Tate; Nadine Thomson, Head of Press and Marketing, Tate; Laura Whitton, Rights and Reproduction and Rose Dempsey, Serpentine Gallery; Helen Dobson, V&A Images; Jo Lightfoot, Laura Willis, Felicity Awdry and Eugenia Bell at Laurence King; Michael Craig-Martin, Michael Rock and Miguel Zugaza; and special thanks to Zara Moore at Pentagram.

Photography Credits

p. 9: V&A Archives, p. 10: Courtesy Olafur Eliasson/Tate Modern, p. 11: The Guggenheim Las Vegas, p. 14: Courtesy Serpentine Gallery, p. 15: Angus Hyland, p. 18: Julian Anderson, p. 21: Courtesy Tate Photography, pp. 23, 24, 107: Rick Dávila/Museo Nacional del Prado, pp. 32, 145: James Shanks, pp. 36: Greger Ulf Nilson, pp. 42, 44: Peter Mauss/ESTO, pp. 48, 50: Nick Turner, p. 52: Gaël Amzalag, pp. 58, 60: Agathe Poupeney, p. 62: Claudio Franzini/Cameraphoto, p. 66: Alessandra Chemollo/ORCH, p. 74: Courtesy Gagosian Gallery, New York. Photograph by Robert McKeever, p. 78: Louis Vignaud (Copyright), p. 86: Peter White, pp. 90, 92, 95: Courtesy Moderna Museet, p. 96: James Kuo (poster designed by Steven Mosier), p. 102: Courtesy of Mori Art Museum, p. 109: Phil Sayer/Museo Nacional del Prado, pp. 112, 114: Armand Mevis, p. 116: Pablo Mason, pp. 119, 131: Courtesy 2x4, pp. 128, 130: Michel Denance, p. 142: Kurt Koepfle, p. 132: Helene Binet, p. 137: Rolant Dafis, p. 138: Courtesy The Photographers' Gallery, p. 146: Nigel Shafran, pp. 152, 154, 157: Gert-Jan van Rooij, pp. 162, 164: Courtesy Vitra Design Museum, p. 166: Cameron Wittig, p. 172: Andrew G Hobbs

NB Sample photography, unless stated otherwise, by Nick Turner.